KEEPER
OF AN ORDINARY

CORT FERNALD

Thanks to S.H. for the invaluable advice and assistance with editing and formatting. Also, thanks to Bridget Lambrecht for proofreading. Author photo courtesy of Torri Pantaleon.

Keeper of an Ordinary/ Cort Fernald. -- 1st edition
ISBN-13: 978-0692485521
ISBN-10: 069248552X

For Ron, Royce, Tielyr and Tony

Chapter 1

A figure caught in the sniper's crosshairs; the prey that never sleeps. Rich closed his notebook, slid the pen in the spiral binding, placing it on the bedside table. He switched off the lamp and gave himself over to the dark. Sleep lightly, he thought, or wake up with a gun in his mouth.

These were the lonely hours, pursued and scared. Dreams of running.

Tires squeal. Glass and metal crashes. The clock numerals glow red...2:13am

A shout in the street. Her angry reply...3:19am

Police car and a pulsing siren...4:07am.

Every hour Rich woke remembering the sensation of fire burning down his side; every hour recollecting the blood pouring all over his legs, reliving his brush with death at the hands of a sniper.

A train whistle blew long, long, and short as Amtrak's eastbound California Zephyr rolled into downtown Omaha.

He opened his eyes to gray lines of light seeping through the slates of the blinds and scanned the large sparsely furnished bedroom. Roommate, his small black on white Boston terrier, lay curled at the bottom of the double bed. The no-brand phone on the bedside table read: 5:58am. In the stillness, Rich could hear the whoosh of cars and rumble of truck traffic along I-80 a half mile north. He would catch that flow of hot metal and burning rubber and never stop. For one minute, he might be safe.

Reaching across he slid his hand under the pillow, gripping the Glock 32. Rich pulled out the black handgun, clicked the safety, yawned and stretched his arms. He grimaced. Pain stung his side.

Roommate woke and struggled up to his feet, snorting and shaking.

"Hey Rooms." Rich cleared his throat.

The dog's tags jangled as he scratched behind his ear.

A slight wind rattled the window in its casement.

Rich swung out of bed, his bare feet landing on the dark stained hardwood floor. He jerked his robe off the hook inside the closet door, tied it and slid the Glock into the pocket. The weight of the gun pulled down the right side of the robe. He scrolled through calls on his phone as he walked through the apartment.

"C'mon Roomy. Bet you need to take a leak."

The terrier leapt off the bed and scampered out the bedroom, into the living room. He ran ahead of Rich, crossing the large room to the kitchen area at the back of the flat. A wood, high back chair stood before a window. On many a sleepless night Rich would sit in his dark apartment, shotgun across his lap, standing vigil staring into the blackness outside. Rich checked the sky through the living room blinds. Overcast clouds hung above the rooftops like any other autumn day. Just to make sure, Rich scanned the pueblo-style auto garage across the street. There was no one there. Roomy circled at the kitchen door as Rich shuffled in, yawning again.

Rich turned into the pantry bending down to a bank of recorders with green lights and a computer. The screen split into four black and white squares showed video from four exterior cameras. The top right screen showed steel mesh stairs to the fenced back area. Rich glanced at the screen with a view of 16th street. A lone woman with a brown shopping bag waited at the bus stop. The bottom screens had two angles from the front along Vinton Street. He studied the top right of the square and dumpster in the corner. He saw no one. Rich lifted the iron bar across the steel back door and turned back the deadbolt.

Roomy stood on his hind legs.

Pulling the Glock from his robe pocket, Rich eased the door open. The little dog darted out onto the landing. Rich did a quick head check around the jamb and watched Roomy jump down step by step. A cold breeze caught him in the face and he ducked back in. He closed the door and stepped back into the pantry. The black and white dog jumped to the gravel parking lot and ran to a grassy area in the corner by the dumpster. Rich slipped the gun into his robe pocket.

Rich filled the coffeemaker and dropped two English muffins in the toaster. He thought he heard Roomy at the door and swung around, hand on the Glock. He leaned into the pantry checking the video screen. The dog sniffed around the dumpster, lifting his leg at the base. With Roomy still busy, he took the dog's bowl from the floor and ladled half a cup of dry food.

The train whistle blew long, short, long, short, as the California Zephyr chugged out of Omaha.

Roommate scratched at the back door. Rich checked the video and saw the little terrier sitting at the closed door.

"Good boy, Roomy," he said, opening the door wide enough to let the dog trot in. He closed the door, twisted the deadbolt and lowered the iron bar. "I've got some breakfast for you." Roommate pranced in going directly to his water bowl on a rubber mat at the foot of the center island. He drank loudly. Rich set the food bowl down. The dog tucked into it, his metal tags clanging against the bowl rim.

In the living room Rich set the phone and Glock on a pile of papers in the center of a round table. A haphazard pyramid of books on the world sex trade, Russian organized crime, Human Trafficking and Prostitution in the Soviet Union and Russian dictionary climbed from the table top. Yellow squares of paper marked pages in the texts. Manila folders and CDs completed the clutter around a laptop. He lifted the lid of a laptop and pressed the power button.

The coffee maker bubbled loudly in the kitchen. The smell of brewing coffee and toasting muffins permeated the flat.

A 42-inch flat screen TV sat on a low console a yard away from the bank of windows. Tangles of cables, cords and wires stretched from outlets and plugs beneath the windows. Pushing papers around Rich found the television remote, clicked on CNN and adjusted the volume to a low mumble while waiting for the laptop to boot up.

The living room exhibited few of the normal creature comforts; worn leather couch the color of a baseball mitt, low coffee table and single chair on a black and gold oriental rug. Dust and grime framed clean squares and rectangles attesting to other lives and other scenes missing from the wall.

In a corner of one wall, a pair of black frames held college diplomas, a bachelor's in journalism from Monmouth College; its companion, a master's in communications from Northwestern University. In another picture a couple grinned to the camera under the long branches of a large Banyan tree in Lahaina, Maui. The woman stood the same height as Rich. She had an athletic build and short honey blonde hair. Pinned next to the picture, a letter from the Pulitzer Committee notified Rich of his nomination. Two dog eared newspaper front pages were tacked next to the letter. The bold headlines crossed the top of the page: State Official in South Town Sex Ring and Russian Mafia Sex Slaves at Suburb Parties. Bylines read: Richard Rice. These were reminders of the life he fled.

Muffins popped in the toaster.

Cherry wood shelves stacked on the wall behind the table. Bose bookcase speakers wired to a CD player and record turntable and portable MP3 player were set amongst an untidy stack of CDs and 45s scattered across the shelves. Books and piles of manila folders littered the other shelves. Kitty corner stood a tall, wide, gray metal, gun safe. The safe resembled a bank vault with black combination tumbler and handle. Rich tossed the television remote onto the table, got up, and picked up the Glock.

In the kitchen Roomy sat before his empty bowl, licking his chops, sneezing and licking. "Doing some chores?" Rich asked him, putting the Glock into his robe pocket. He took down a coffee cup from a cabinet. "On today's agenda is a bank run," he informed the little dog.

"And then...maybe we can go and..." Rich stopped, knowing the dog knew *walk* and would get excited. "Don't worry, I got you covered."

Roommate followed Rich as he crossed to the back of the pantry. He went to a padlocked half door with a hinged slot on an old dumb waiter. On the floor lay a dirty off white canvas bag. Rich snatched the bag from the floor and tucked it under his arm. Just before turning, he jerked the padlocked handle, checking the catch and the lock. Rich took the buttered muffins and coffee into the living room and set them on the table.

Dropping the bag on the table, sighing, sitting, Rich put the Glock next to the bag. "We'll do a check downstairs later," he told the dog. He logged on as Keeper 1X and opened the time card application spreadsheet.

Cleaning staff (Carmelita Ruiz, Rosella Ruiz) in at 9am and out at 10:30am.

Jorge Ruiz logged in at 11am; out at 2pm, in at 3:30pm and out at 9:12pm.

Tom Waller timed in at 6pm and out at 2am. Rich knew Tom probably worked more hours, but by the clock he was in and out in 8 hours.

Daisy Lincoln logged in at 1pm and out at 9pm.

Rich shook out the collection of cash, coins and credit card receipts from the canvas bag. He thumbed through the paper-clipped credit card receipts, making sure all were signed. Clicking on a bookkeeping application opened a second spreadsheet, dated yesterday. Tom had all the transactions totaled including credit and debit cards. At the bottom of the tab Tom wrote a rundown of the evening shift. "Slow night. No problems. Number four pull needs gas." Popping the rest of the muffin in his mouth and taking a drink of coffee, Rich keyed in the tallies from Wednesday.

Gisele Esslin, owner of record for The Ordinary, had set up the bookkeeping application, a no-brainer. "Numbers first," she told Rich over and over. This didn't sink in until he screwed up a payday and had some pissed off employees. He realized he had a responsibility to them. They had bills. They relied on him. He failed them but luckily did not lose very good employees. Gisele almost drove down from Chicago. But instead set up his books application and sent it over as an email attachment. Now all facets of the business, from employee times, to stock and supplies, vendor accounts and accounts payable and receivables were electronic. If it could be, it would be on the computer. Once Rich finished the books he opened his Tor browser mail service and attached a copy to Gisele.

He clicked SEND on the Telegram encrypted email and locked the computer.

A Route 7 downtown bus growled loudly up 16th street, startling Rich. His hand shook. "Dammit," he whispered under his breath. "Pay attention."

"Okay, Rooms," he said standing. "I'm going to shave and shower, then we'll check downstairs." He spun the tumbler on the gun safe, left, left, right, left. It clicked and he jerked the handle, pulling back the heavy door. The safe held an array of weaponry: a pair of shotguns, Browning Stalker pump and a sawed off, a Springfield 1903 bolt action rifle and Remington model 1911A1. He had inherited these from his dad. Tacked next to the Springfield was a yellowing 8x10 photo of his dad sitting in a rickshaw in front of the Saigon Hilton. He wore ODs with no insignias, sleeves rolled and boonie hat. Grinning, Rich's dad cradled the Springfield and wore the .45 as a sidearm. In fading blue ink on the bottom of the photo was written: Operation Shoofly 1962-Paris of the Orient. A silver Smith and Wesson .38, his small carry gun, hung on a hook. Tear gas and pepper spray and boxes of ammo, from 30-06, .38 and .45 caliber to .357 and .223 rounds stacked the shelves. Bandoleers of 12 pellet buckshot hung from the safe door. Nearly invisible in the corner, leaned a Bushmaster M4 carbine. Not his favorite weapon, Rich took the M4 to the range often. All plastic and video game good looks, Rich preferred the wood and iron weight of the older weapons. He tossed the canvas bag in the safe, slammed the door and spun the tumbler. He kept the Glock with him.

"You want to come along?"

The bathroom branched off the bedroom in the front of the flat. Coffee in hand, gun in pocket, Rich went into the black and white tiled bathroom. He held the door for Roomy trotting after, then locked it and set the chain. He placed the Glock on the towel shelf behind him. He could turn, or could reach it from the shower. Roomy settled on the bathroom rug and watched with much curiosity. Hanging his robe on the hook next to the door as the sink filled with hot water for his shave. Rich studied himself in the mirror above the basin. He appeared haggard, in need of a full night's sleep. Others had said he bore a slight resemblance to the actor Steve McQueen. He kept his sandy brown hair closely cropped and had a similar expressive, mobile mouth and steady blue eyes; as well as the rough-hewn masculine cuteness of the actor. He didn't see it, but had come to accept the compliment with a half shrug and shy smile. He stayed fit, in decent shape for his mid-forties. He'd been working out more urgently and his lanky frame had become taut and lean. Twisting to the left he saw the long scar cut diagonally in a downward line from his right shoulder blade to his belly button. Reddish, wide and still sensitive to the touch, it reminded Rich how close the sniper's bullet had come. He would not dwell on it.

He shaved and drew back the clear plastic shower curtain, stepping under the scalding water. Soaping and rinsing, he got in and out as quickly as he could.

Toweling off, slapping on Calvin Klein *Euphoria* aftershave on his cheeks and neck, Rich then unlocked the bath and went into the bedroom. Placing the Glock on the dresser, he picked out a black t-shirt and slipped on a pair of faded Lee jeans. He knelt and clapped his hands for Roommate to come. The little dog huffed and licked Rich's hands as he scratched behind its ears.

Rich stood at the second floor window, cup of hot coffee in hand looking down at the street.

Omaha World-Herald broadsheets borne on an updraft, rose magically from the intersection of 16th street and Vinton. The long prow of the sign lettered The Ordinary, Public House jutted out from the second floor of the Italianate colonial red brick building. A banner below the sign flapped: Husker Football-Saturday.

Relentless winds pushing out of Rocky Mountains into the Nebraska panhandle, over the western sand hills and across the central plains bent autumn stalks of dried up yellow corn to the force of the moving air. Boiling gray blue clouds hang low and trailed the eastward gusts. Red and orange leaves plucked from thin limbs by the breeze tumbled down to the ground and piled in gutters and curbs. A strong wind swirled through the old Packing Town into the Missouri Valley and followed the southerly twists of the blue river. The breeze swarmed up behind the brave few bundled in red Nebraska sweatshirts hurrying along the sidewalks. Though new to South Omaha, Rich knew the wind had the bite of winter's approach.

Roomy bounded onto the couch, circled and circled, then settled down.

Rich scrutinized each parked car along the street. It gave him little ease seeing no vehicles with blue on white Illinois license plates.

"Helluva way to live," he said, turning away from the window. "C'mon Rooms, let's check downstairs." The dog's head popped up.

Tucking the Glock into his back pocket and scooping up cash from the table, Rich patted his leg to get Roommate to follow. In the pantry, he sorted through his key ring and found the key to open the steel door on the dumb waiter. The door squeaked open revealing a dark shaft with ladder on the back wall. It ran the length of the dumb waiter, from the roof and down two floors to the basement. Rich, with Roomy under his arm, stepped across the shaft to the ladder. He grabbed a rung with his free hand and started down. The dog looked up and down, but remained calm in Rich's embrace.

At the first floor, Rich stepped off and set Roommate down. The little dog took off after all the new smells. Next to the dumb waiter a large wood frame and chicken wire store room had stacks of cans, boxes, linen and bar towels, glasses and dishware. Rich walked into the bar kitchen. Jorge kept the kitchen spotless, with gleaming stainless steel counters, shelves, griddle, fryer and sink. Bread and buns were stacked in a glass cabinet. A large refrigerating unit hummed at the end of a counter. The garbage cans were empty with new plastic bags. A pet peeve of Rich's.

Jorge's wife Carmelita and sister-in-law Rosella, the cleaning crew, were scheduled to come in at nine.

Roomy's tags jangled as he darted across the dimly lit bar.

The top half of the windows and glowing security lights illuminated the bar. The bottom banks of windows were painted black and below this were a series of wooden booths with table and benches. A small stage area in the corner couldn't have held two turntables and a microphone or more than a three-piece band, close. Circular tables scattered throughout the bar. A long polished mahogany bar and stools ran along the wall opposite the windows. A large mirror with glass shelves filled with multicolored bottles backed the bar. Two glass-fronted coolers, one with wine bottles, the other with a variety of bottled beers, flanked the mirror.

Roommate sniffed along the back wall, on the trail of something.

"Attaboy, Rooms," Rich said, lifting the drop leaf and going behind the bar. He walked up and back, checking for empties, napkins or any garbage. Tom didn't clean at closing time. In the sink Rich saw an empty green O'Doul's bottle. "Well," he thought. "I owe him more than that." In the center of the bar Rich checked the taps. One, two, three were in good shape, but tap four sputtered and ran slow. Tom was right; it needed gas.

Rich booted up the computer and put the opening cash in the register.

"Rooms?" Rich called, coming out from behind the bar. "What're you into?"

The dog trotted up.

"C'mon buddy, we have to go down to the basement." Rich lifted Rooms, went to the back and started down the dumb waiter. The little dog started squirming, looking anxiously at Rich.

"I know...you don't like it down here."

Rich set the dog down. Roommate didn't move, warily glancing left and right.

Shafts of light came in from dirty half windows at street level. Dust drifted through the light. Discarded mattresses and bed frames heaped in a corner. Boxes of supplies, stacks of old chairs and tables, piles of wood and miscellany littered the basement. It smelled of old wood, stale booze, oil and damp. The furnace with a maze of shiny ducting in various sizes went into the ceiling and all over. A 2x4 and plywood framed structure held beer kegs, canisters of gas and hoses going up into the ceiling.

Roommate whimpered at Rich's feet.

"Okay tough guy. Give me a minute." Rich popped the gas line on the old canister and rolled it aside. He wrestled a new canister into the holder, pushed on the hose and spun the faucet. It hissed a moment, then went silent. Rich pulled out his phone and made a note to call the gas vendor.

"Tell me, Rooms," Rich picked up the dog and stepped over debris to the dumb waiter. "How the hell did you get up to the second floor that night?"

They climbed. As they climbed past the first floor, Rich heard a vacuum cleaner. Jorge's wife and sister in law were busy cleaning the bar. Upstairs, Rich let Roommate loose, then closed and locked the dumb waiter door. He went back into the living room and picked up the remote. He turned the volume louder when the picture of an old man appeared on the screen with the headline: Convicted Illinois Official dead.

"Illinois' former top educator has been found hanged in his cell at Statesville Prison. Samuel Decker, 83-years old, ex-director of Illinois Higher Education, awaited sentencing for crimes that shocked Chicago and its South Suburbs, and had repercussions halfway around the world to Russia. CNN Reporter Marie Bracket is on the scene at Statesville."

Rich sank into a chair, watching.

"Thank you, Deborah. Samuel Decker faced sentencing for multiple counts of kidnap and rape. Decker, his son Rod, a suburban real estate mogul, and two others were convicted of crimes that spanned nearly 30 years. A murder conviction involving a Des Moines resident Michael Smith is on appeal. Smith, investigated Decker and was killed in a suspicious auto accident."

The reporter glanced down at her notes.

"Smith left behind a detailed notebook implicating Decker and the others, as well as members of Russian organized crime in Chicago. Smith's notes were used by Chicago Tribune reporters for a series of exposes detailing the Decker's rape parties and Russian mafia's sex trade and human trafficking."

"Don't say it, lady," Rich murmured.

"The exposes earned Tribune reporters a Pulitzer nomination and may have been the impetus for an unknown gun man shooting Park Forest Daily reporter Richard Rice."

Rich tensed and threw his fists in the air. "No...no."

"Rice was shot and at first reported killed. But then he disappeared."

"Thanks." Rich grumbled, clicking off the TV.

Every time his career started to take off, the backhand of fate would slap him silly. Rich's investigative reports got him in the door at the Tribune. That's when the 3am phone calls started. Anonymous women's voices with eastern European accents would shout as he sleepily answered.

"Stop your lies or else." The message would vary but the threat remained constant. "Stop writing or else." Rich ignored the calls. He couldn't ignore the black sedan with tinted windows parked across the street. His car and then Gisele's car, were keyed. A brick shattered the windshield. Park Forest police did little. They implied Rich was doing the damage himself, for publicity.

Someone tried to break into the house.

And then the shooting.

Rich opened the gun safe and traded out the Glock for the Smith and Wesson .38. He flipped open and spun the five-round chamber, then clipped an inside the waistband holster on his hip. He holstered and secured the gun and took out the bank bag. The gun safe slammed as Rich closed it, jiggling the lever. He slipped on a hooded sweatshirt and made sure it covered the revolver.

"Bank run, Rooms." The little dog ran up to Rich. "And we'll take a walk after." With the word *walk* Roomy started jumping up on his hind legs.

"Rup...Rup...Rup."

Checking the surveillance cameras on the pantry computer, Rich noted nothing unusual in the lot. He raised the iron bar and unlocked the back door. Roommate raced out the door and hopped down the mesh steel steps. Rich turned back, locked the dead bolt and gave the steel door a shake.

Rich unlocked his black Ford F-150 Heavy Duty with the button on the key fob. He pulled open the door and tossed the bank bag onto the seat. Reaching down he scooped up Roommate. The dog's little legs walked in air before Rich set him on the seat. He jumped over the console and settled in the passenger seat. Rich climbed in and closed the door. He opened the glove box and pulled out the gate opener. The chain link gate slowly wound aside as Rich started up the truck.

Roommate stood with his hind legs on the seat and fore paws on the dashboard. His bulging black eyes darted left then right as Rich eased the truck out the gravel parking lot. At the end of the lot, just before turning onto 16th street, Rich clicked the remote, closing the gate. He watched in the rearview mirror and didn't turn until it was closed.

"Sit back Rooms, you're going to fall."

They drove up 16th street amid light mid-morning traffic and reached the bank. Rich pulled into one of the bays. He stopped and lowered the window, reaching out to take a plastic canister from the pneumatic tube.

"Good morning," a female voice came over the loudspeaker. The heavy Eastern European accent startled Rich. "My name is Ivana..."

"You a new hire?" Rich interrupted, taking the .38 from its holster.

"Yes," she replied.

"Are you Russian?"

"Belarus. How did you...?"

"Hold on, Rooms." Rich jammed the plastic canister back in its holder. He jerked the gearshift to D, stomped on the accelerator, squealing tires and throwing smoke as he roared out the bank bay. He scanned his mirrors left and right and swerved onto L Street, speeding away. Once clear and sure no one followed, Rich slowed.

"We'll go to the branch on 96th," he told Roommate.

At the 96th street branch Rich parked his truck and took the bank bag into the branch. The black and white dog jumped over and sat at the driver's seat, watching. Inside, Rich glanced around, and then went up to the teller counter. He slid the deposit slip and canvas bag to a young woman.

"Good morning," she smiled.

Rich nodded, his hand hanging loose on the revolver side.

The young woman keyed in the amounts and printed out a receipt. "Is there anything else I can do for you, Mr. Keeper?"

"No," Rich said quietly, pocketing the receipt, picking up the empty canvas bag. He stepped back.

"Thank you," she said as Rich turned for the door.

Rich shooed Roomy off the driver's seat. "Move over." He settled in, turned over the engine and heard his phone beep. A text came up from Paul Bertoloni. "Call me," it read.

Rich keyed in Bertoloni's number, then turned at the intersection.

"FBI, Omaha."

"Yeah, connect me to agent Paul Bertoloni, please."

"And who's calling?"

"Rich Rice. He called me."

"I'll put you through."

The line went silent.

"Bertoloni."

"Paul? It's Rich Rice. You wanted me to call?"

"Yeah, thanks for calling back. Can we meet next week?"

"What's up?"

"Not much. You doing all right?"

"This got something to do with old man Decker dying?"

"You saw that, huh? A bit, yeah."

"What time?"

"How about 11?"

"Sure. I open the bar at 11."

"Okay. I'll let you know. Make it on Monday."

"Thanks, Paul."

Rich clicked off the phone and slipped it into his pocket.

"What the hell's going on Roomy? I don't trust that guy." The dog stretched over and licked Rich's face. "Let's get your walk in."

From behind the gun safe, Rich pulled a canvas fishing rod case and unzipped it. He pushed five 12 gauge shotgun rounds into the magazine and slipped the sawed off pump into the case, adding a box of shells and zipping it closed. Rich tucked his notebook under his arm.

"Got to open the bar." He went over and scratched the dog's head. "I'll check on you in a few hours."

Rich climbed down the dumb waiter to the bar. Jorge whistled while setting up the kitchen.

"Morning, Jorge," Rich called, walking through the kitchen.

"*Hola, Jefe*," he responded.

Cleaned, the bar looked and smelled less like a boozer than it ought. Rich ducked under the bar leaf and came up behind. He unzipped the case and leaned it upright under the bar. If he needed he could reach down and come up firing. Bar towels, coasters, napkins, iced mugs, bowls of popcorn Rich did by rote. He powered up two big screen TVs mounted in the back and next to the stage, then lit up the outside surveillance cameras.

"What's on the menu today?"

Jorge came into the bar wiping his hands on a towel. Wiry, though bow-legged Jorge stood medium height and wore a sleeveless white t-shirt with boot cut black jeans. The story of his life was inked up and down either of his spindly arms. Fine line black profiles of his three daughters were interspersed with blotchy prison tats and a full color depiction of the Virgin of Guadalupe. A hair net knotted at the top of his forehead kept his thick jet black hair in place.

"Burritos, tacos: chicken, beef or fish. Quesadillas and the usual burgers or mini pizza. We got a spicy tortilla soup or chicken soup...with a salad or half a sandwich."

"Sounds good, *amigo*." Rich crossed to the small stage and powered up the sound system.

"What're we listening to today?" Jorge asked.

"I'm in a fifties mood." Rich absentmindedly replied, programming the computer mp3 player and mixer. The opening notes of Bennie Spellman's *Lipstick Traces* clanged loudly through the bar. "Wow, volume's up pretty high. What was Tom playing last night?"

"He dint wake you upstairs?"

"Naw, I slept on and off."

"Hendrix...all night long."

Rich chuckled, crossing to the front door. A dry-erase board on a sidewall by the door advertised Mod/Northern Soul Night with DJ, Tuesday Poetry Slam, Big Beat Marathon, Football Saturday and Sunday. He unlocked the door and raised a tinted screen.

"Cafe, *Jefe*?"

"You bet," Rich yelled back as he hefted a Lunch Special sign outside and set it up on the sidewalk. He checked up and down the street. An old brown female pit bull mix with long dangling dugs, trotted up the middle of

Vinton Street. Come back, honey, Rich thought, my Roommate would like to meet you.

"Your cafe, Keeper."

"*Gracias*, Jorge."

Rich settled on a high stool in the back corner of the bar and opened his notebook.

Four men in stained work overalls walked in. They waved to Jorge as they took seats at a table. Rich grabbed four menus and came around the bar.

"Something to drink, gentlemen?" He handed each a laminated menu. They reeked of the abattoir.

"*Si*, Bud light." The others nodded.

"*Quatro* Bud Light?"

"*Si.*"

"*Gracias.* Jorge will take your order."

Rich ducked behind the bar, pulled four draughts of Bud Light and opened a ticket on the computer. He placed the beers on a circular tray and set it on the corner of the bar. Jorge came out from the kitchen and took the tray.

"Ticket in?"

"Yeah, got the beers on it."

Other patrons straggled in, shaking from the outside chill.

The Coasters' *Youngblood* played low under the conversation throughout the bar. Billiard balls clanked in a side room.

"Hey, Keeper?" an older man shouted from the end of the bar. "How long you been here?"

"Who, me? Or the bar?"

"The bar."

"About three months." Rich walked down and leaned on the bar.

"And what's the name of this place?

"The Ordinary," Rich said, grinning.

"See I told you. The sign wasn't wrong." He chided an even older man sitting next to him. "This here's Bennie."

"How do Bennie. They call me Keeper."

"Nice to meet you...but why Ordinary?"

"You'd have to ask the owner. She lives in Chicago," Rich said. "I just work here. But I think it's from colonial days. Bars were called public houses because folks turned their downstairs into a tavern. That's especially true for houses along the carriage routes." The two men drank and listened intently. "The public houses were ordinary residences. The owners were known as Keepers of an Ordinary."

"So this is someone's house?"

"Well, no. But people do live upstairs."

"Oh yeah...who?"

"I think there's a black family that lives upstairs."

"So that's why it's called The Ordinary?"

"I would've never known."

"Another round?"

"Naw, we gotta get back to the plant."

"Yup," Bennie drained his glass. "Back to the killing floor." He slapped a ten-dollar bill on the bar. "We'll see ya, Keeper."

"All right, gentlemen." Rich waved as they tottered out.

Activity slowed after lunch with a few couples and groups coming in for a drink or something to munch. At two o'clock Jorge closed the kitchen and cleaned up. His schedule gave him three hours off and then he returned for the dinner hours. He readied to leave. Two Omaha cops, one fat and one skinny, strolled in. They stood in the entrance and swept the room with their eyes. Rich checked the surveillance camera and saw a black and white patrol car parked out front.

"Afternoon, gentlemen."

"You Keeper?"

"I am. Can I get you a Coke? Coffee?"

"I'd like a coffee."

"I'm good," the skinny cop said.

"Jorge?" Rich called. "Any coffee left in the pot?"

Jorge stuck his head around the corner. "For Omaha's finest? You betcha."

The two cops sat, squirming onto bar stools.

"Just opened, did you?"

"About three months ago."

Jorge brought out a mug of coffee. He hesitated, reaching at arm's length placing the coffee and nudging it near the cop. Both cops looked him over. Nervously, he smiled placing a small plate with a single doughnut next to the coffee and backed away.

"I'm...I'm out of here, *Jefe*."

"Okay," Rich replied. "I'll see you in a couple of hours."

"Funny guy." The fat cop said pushing away the doughnut.

"I'll have it if you don't want it." The skinny cop reached across and plucked the doughnut from the plate.

"We have something for you, Keeper," the fat cop said.

"Oh yeah?" Rich stepped back from the bar, moving his right hand slowly behind.

A cop took out an envelope from his shirt pocket and slapped it on the bar. KEEPER was written in black letters.

Rich didn't pick it up.

"Relax," the skinny cop added. "Lt. Lavender asked us to drop it off."

"And also to let you know we'll be patrolling the neighborhood."

"Lavender? You're shitting me?"

"Yeah, Lavender. I shit you not."

Rich tore open the envelope. A business card was clipped to a note from Lt. Lawrence Lavender. He read quickly. Lavender introduced himself and let Rich know he would be at an upcoming meeting at the FBI office on Monday.

"We'll be in touch," the chubby cop said, struggling off the bar stool. "And about your cook..."

"What about my cook?"

The cop grinned. "He makes a hellacious cup of coffee."

"That he does," Rich muttered watching the cops saunter out.

Chapter 2

A black wrought iron fence surrounded the nondescript white panel and tinted glass three-story structure occupying the western corner of the busy intersection of 120th at I Street. No sign, no logo, gave any indication of what the building housed. A driveway turned to a white guardhouse and orange striped gate.

Rich wheeled his truck into the entrance and eased to a stop before the gate.

No one occupied the guardhouse. A weathered paper sign taped over a small speaker read: Press Red Button and Speak.

Rich hesitated, scanning his mirrors and checking over his right shoulder. Assured he hadn't been followed, he pressed the button.

"Federal Bureau of Investigation," a male voice squawked out the speaker. "How can I help you?"

"My name is Richard Rice. I have an appointment with agent Paul Bertoloni."

The engine in Rich's truck idled as he waited.

"I have confirmation from agent Bertoloni, Mr. Rice." The gate slowly rose. "Follow the arrows to the parking area in the front. An officer will meet you."

"Okay, thanks." Rich pulled the gearshift to Drive.

Rich followed the arrows and parked between two gray sedans. Chain link fencing partitioned the parking area. Surveillance cameras in the corners watched Rich as he got out and locked his truck.

Two security officers in black uniforms approached.

"Mr. Rice?" One had a radio in his hand. "Are you carrying any weapons, sir?"

"Yes." Rich unclipped his .38 and handed it to the officer. "I want that back."

"Certainly. When you leave. Carrying any other weapons?"

"No."

"Open the truck, please." The second officer had a long handled mirror and circled around the truck checking underneath.

"Sure." The locks clicked.

"Any weapons or explosives in the truck?" Before Rich could answer, the officer peered in and felt under the seats. "You can lock it...and follow me."

Rich trailed the officers through the entrance where another security officer with a handheld metal detecting electronic wand asked him to stop.

"Hold your hands up, please."

"Step forward."

The officer with the wand went up and down Rich's legs and arms. The wand squealed at Rich's belly.

"Raise your t-shirt, please."

He complied.

"It's your belt buckle."

An officer handed Rich a clipboard. "Please fill this out." Rich signed his name, date, time and Bertoloni as his appointment. As he signed, the officer passed him a visitor badge on an orange lanyard.

"An officer will accompany you to the second floor."

"Thanks." Rich opened the door to a gray marble lobby where the large blue and gold shield of the FBI decorated the wall above chrome lettering: Federal Bureau of Investigation, Omaha Division. An American flag and state of Nebraska flag stood in the corner by a potted palm. Rich crossed to a row of elevators with the officer behind him. A harried looking woman with a shifting armful of manila folders hustled up. Her heels clacked across the marble floor. Two white-haired men in dark blue suits rounded a corner. They glanced at the security officer and Rich. Their conversation hushed while they waited for the elevator.

"What floor?" Rich asked, entering the elevator with the officer.

"Two please," the woman replied, brushing back a stray strand of brown hair. "Thanks."

"Third floor," one of the white haired men said.

Pressing the second and third floor buttons the doors closed. The five rode up in distracted silence.

When the doors parted for the second floor, the woman gave Rich a quick glance and smile as she hurried out.

As Rich stepped out the two men started talking behind. The security officer followed.

Frosted glass partitions and gleaming wood veneer separated the cubicles and tables of the large office area. A glass enclosed conference room lay to the right of the elevator, at the end of a short hall. Seated at the head of a long table agent Bertoloni sorted through papers and tapped on a tablet. Rich pushed open the conference room door.

"Paul."

"Rich," Bertoloni looked up.

"Tell your babysitter he can turn me loose."

"It's okay, officer. I'll notify you when he's ready to leave."

"Yes sir."

Rich went around the table. They shook hands and he sat to Bertoloni's left.

"How have you been, Rich?"

"Still alive."

Paul Bertoloni couldn't have been more than 30 years old, tall and with a fair complexion, not as Italian looking as his surname implied. He wore a navy blue suit with gray shirt and navy blue tie with a large red letter N tie tack.

"Anything happen lately?"

"Naw. We're still cool." Rich settled into the tall leather chair, his back to the wall, across from the glass entrance. "Omaha PD sent a couple of uniforms to the bar, scared the hell out of my cook."

"If you hired legals..."

"Jorge's legal."

"That's not what I meant."

"I know what you meant and I would trust Jorge more than those old timers on the Omaha PD."

"They went out to tell you Lavender would be at this meeting."

"Lavender?"

"Yeah, Lavender." They traded smiles. "C'mon, none of us get to pick our names."

"But we can change them."

Cursing and clattering out in the hallway drew Rich's attention. There, a short, fattish man, in white shirt and tie scrambled about on all fours picking up papers that had fallen out of his open attaché case. The man's black rim glasses were askew. He wore his reddish blond hair closely cropped.

"Lavender?" Rich tilted his head.

Bertoloni glanced over. "Uh huh."

Hugging an attaché case and papers, flushed and breathless, Lavender butted open the glass conference door.

"Agent Bertoloni?" he panted. He had a squeaky almost falsetto voice.

"Yes."

"Oh good. I'm in the right place." Lavender dropped his case and papers onto the table. He collapsed in a chair. The knot of his tie was twisted sideways. The orange lanyard from his visitors badge tangled with his Omaha PD badge dangling off his shirt pocket. Large wet circles were under each arm, and beads of sweat rolled down his temples. "Is this Mr. Keeper?" Lavender motioned toward Rich.

Bertoloni slowly turned to Rich.

"Oh, just call me Keeper." Rich leaned back, smirking.

Paul tapped his pen on the pile of papers. "We have a lot to cover and maybe we should start with introductions."

They sat quiet.

The agent sighed. "Detective, would you mind?"

"Me? Oh, sure." Lavender drew himself up. "Larry Lavender, Detective Lt. Omaha police, special unit."

"Agent Paul Bertoloni, FBI, Omaha."

"Keeper, bar owner, Omaha."

"No no no," Bertoloni said, throwing his pen down. "For real, Rich."

"Okay," Rich smiled. "I'm Richard, Rich, Richie...don't call me Dick, Rice. I run a bar in South Omaha." He studied Lavender. "Before that I was journalist for the Park Forest Daily, a Chicago Tribune newspaper."

"Close your mouth, detective."

"So you're not Mr. Keeper?"

"Oh no, he is," Bertoloni replied.

"That's a name I use."

"I'm confused." Lavender's eyes went from Bertoloni to Rich.

"C'mon, Rich. We have a lot of new information to get to and we need Detective Lavender up-to-speed."

Lavender looked expectantly at Rich, while Rich had a nagging feeling about the detective. Not a trust issue, more of a question of competence.

"A little over a year ago I met Mike Smith, a classmate of my editor, Bill More, at the Park Forest Daily. The Daily is a suburban edition of the Chicago Tribune. Smith was a sad case. His wife was raped and murdered the previous year and he never got over it."

"That's still an open case," Bertoloni interrupted.

"They're never going to find out who did that to his wife. But at a class reunion, Smith learned of the abduction and rape of his high school girlfriend. He became obsessed with finding who raped his high school girlfriend. A psychiatrist would call it generalized behavior. Smith thought if he found those who raped his girlfriend he was also finding who raped and murdered his wife. But there was something fatalistic going on with that guy. Like he knew the more he dug the more likely it was he would be killed.

"He sniffed around and his investigation led to a character named Sam Decker, an Illinois state official, his son Rod Decker, a real estate tycoon and a banker. These guys had ties to Bratva in Chicago. Smith got killed in a suspicious auto accident. But he left a notebook of his investigation and I followed up, writing articles that appeared in the Daily and Tribune. The Deckers were convicted of multiple counts of kidnap, rape and trafficking in human beings." Rich took a breath. "Later on they were convicted of the murder of Mike Smith."

"Decker?" Lavender's face screwed up. "That name sounds familiar."

"It should." Rich said. "Old man Decker was found hanged in his cell in prison. He was awaiting sentencing."

"So what's the problem?"

"The problem isn't Decker or the others. It's his friends, the Bratva."

"Bratva?" Lavender asked.

"Russian Mafia."

"After the convictions," Bertoloni picked up the explanation. "Threats started. Phone calls late at night. A break-in at Rich's house. And it culminated in a sniper taking a shot at Rich. Luckily, they missed. Well, it tore up Rich's right side."

Rich raised his eyebrows. "Yeah...lucky me."

"Sorry, Rich," Bertoloni shrugged.

Rich turned to Lavender. "The threatening callers had Russian accents. And mostly young girls. The day I was shot Chicago PD told me to get out of town, saying it would blow over in a year or so. I sent my wife away and...."

"Where'd she go?"

Rich glared at him.

"I mean you," Lavender stammered. "You came to Omaha."

"You don't need to know that, Lieutenant." Bertoloni interceded.

"But if..."

"No," Rich leaned forward. "You don't need to know where she is, or anything about her. Okay?" He emphasized each word slowly.

"Easy now. Six months ago Rich arrived in Omaha. He bought a building and set up The Ordinary about four months ago."

Lavender settled back in his chair and stretched out his arms, exposing his wet arm pits. "I guess I'm up to speed now."

Rich glanced away and sighed.

"Should I be taking notes?"

"No, no notes," Bertoloni said. "There are developments. And some new players." He touched his tablet. "Let me put this up on the screen." Bertoloni connected to a terminal, as a white screen descended from the ceiling behind him. "Sorry, guys. Anybody need something to drink?"

"Not me," Rich said.

"I'd like a Dr. Pepper."

The agent pointed to a half-size refrigerator in a corner across the conference room. "Help yourself. There should be some soft drinks in there."

Lavender got up.

"And catch the lights, please."

"No problem." Lavender bent down and rummaged through the fridge.

"Lavender?" Rich called out. "On second thought, if there's a water, I'll take one."

"You got it, bud." Lavender underhanded a bottle of water to Rich.

"Thanks."

Lavender opened the can of soda, drank and walked back to his seat, flicking off the lights on the way.

A broad-faced, small-mouthed woman, stout with heft and no curves appeared on the screen. Her short orange hair appeared disheveled, spiked on top. She had cruel black passionless eyes, as if weighing life and death was like picking lint off her sleeve. Dressed in heavy cloth of gray and black, her clothing hung on her like loose burlap.

"This is Irina Ilyich Franko, alias Suka," Bertoloni said. "Suka originates from Southern Palmira, also known as Odessa. She matriculated with the Bratva in and around the Ukraine and Crimea with *Malina*, the Odessa Mafia."

"What a babe," Lavender said.

"That babe is now the chief of the Russian mafia's sex and human trafficking operations in the United States. The Madam of the Madams. It's been a long, hard climb for Suka. And she's built it on a mountain of bodies." The agent paused. "Ever run across her in your research?"

"I did," Rich replied. "My sources had her in Toronto, transporting girls through Detroit."

"A lot of the mafia members in the former Soviet immigrated to the U.S. under the Jackson-Vanik Amendment. More background. Suka came to the pre-Bratva *vory v zakone* via her father, Ivan Dimitri Franko, who Stalin threw into a gulag in the late thirties. Irina inherited the name Suka from her father."

"I'm sorry," Lavender asked. "Her father was named Suka?"

"Not really. Suka means *bitch* in Russian. Stalin offered early release from the gulags if members of the *vory* fought Hitler. Most *vory* refused. They'd have nothing to do with the government. But Ivan Dimitri took the opportunity to get out of the gulag. Can't say I blame him. He immediately deserted. Nonetheless, the rest of the *vory* branded him Suka."

"I know a little of the Ukrainian character," Rich interjected. "Irina took the name Suka to honor her father and stick it up the noses of the *vory*."

"Also typical of the *vory*," Bertoloni added. "Ivan Dimitri became KGB in the sixties."

"So she was Odessa Mafia while Pops was KGB?"

"That's about right, Lieutenant. He ended upstairs in Lubyanka rather than a guest in a prison cell downstairs."

Bertoloni tapped the tablet and a blurry photo came up of Suka in a room of half-dressed young girls. "Odessa Mafia is known for smuggling and human trafficking. Suka started out as a brothel attendant and moved to kidnapping and then negotiator in the sale of the girls. She had a knack for getting the lowest price from the kidnappers and the highest price from the pimps, be they in Tel Aviv, Frankfurt or New York."

Lavender, wearing an extremely distressed expression, stared at the grainy photo.

"You okay, Detective?"

"No, I mean, yes." He turned away from the photo and wiped his brow. "I have a daughter the same age as those girls."

Rich's eyes narrowed, regarding the lieutenant. Under the column, this-guy-may-be-all right, Rich ticked one for Lavender.

"But I'm not really following this," he complained. "The Russian mafia is not that prominent in Omaha. We've had some young thugs come up from Kansas City and run scams on the Mexican workers in the packing plants. They did some internet fraud schemes on the local banks and insurance companies. Omaha has always been a liquor and gambling town since the thirties under Cowboy Jim. But widespread prostitution? I haven't seen it taking root in Omaha."

"Last year, Omaha PD busted a prostitution ring working out of a gentlemen's club downtown."

"All those girls had Turkish passports. We handed them over to ICE."

"Because the girls were bought from a Turkish pimp. The girls were kidnapped from Moldavia, Ukraine and Serbia."

"What's the going rate for a human being these days?" Rich asked.

"In greenbacks? About $3000 to $4000."

"That's a lot of money." Lavender seemed dumbfounded.

"Not really. Each of those girls will make that back in two to three days. Human trafficking has a better turnover than drugs and less emphasis by law enforcement."

"The Russians don't have a big footprint in Omaha—so I'm not sure why I am here."

"You're here for him." Bertoloni pointed to Rich. "His articles on the Decker's sex ring put a lot of heat on Bratva's Chicago activities. They had upscale brothels on the Gold Coast and North Shore. Paid off cops, judges and politicians protected them. Those boys ran when the stories hit print. Rich's investigation crippled Bratva."

"So we're supposed to help him?"

"No, keep him alive." Bertoloni worked his tablet. "From this guy." A picture flashed up on the screen. "This character is Suka's son Nikolai Franko."

Suka's narrow-faced son looked middle-aged and wore a long powder blue drape coat, with black velvet collar, black velvet pocket flaps and string tie. His trousers were tight, also black and pegged down to an oversized thick sole pair of blue suede shoes.

"Looks like Elvis," Lavender said.

Nikolai had long slicked up black hair combed into a high rounded pompadour. His sideburns were grown out and trimmed at his jaw line.

"Not a bad analogy."

"I've seen him before," Rich said.

"Nikolai is the result of a South Florida tryst with Bratva arms merchant Luddy 'Tarzan' Fainberg."

"Suka mates with Tarzan and out pops Elvis."

"He likes to call himself Nicky...Nicky Franko and he's a torpedo. He has a Madonna and child tattooed across his back, Bratva stars on each shoulder and is said to laugh like a snake."

"What does that mean?"

"Do snakes laugh?"

"Just reading what's on the dossier. Rich?" Agent Bertoloni turned. "We're a thousand percent certain Nicky Franko was the shooter that nearly got you."

"Well, I wouldn't call him a good shot," Lavender added, smiling at Rich.

Rich stared back. His foot tapped. Shoulders tensed. This meeting headed south fast.

"And that's the thing." Bertoloni leaned forward. "At first Suka believed Rich was shot and killed. But our informants are telling us they aren't so sure now. No death notice was filed or published."

"You're keeping tabs on Nicky, right?"

Bertoloni glanced down, silent.

"You don't know where the hell he is, do you?"

"His last known whereabouts was in Chicago."

"If I knew where Nicky was I'd go after him."

"We want these guys to come after you."

"You what?"

Bertoloni's eyes panicked. "No...no." He held up both hands, palms out. "I said that wrong. We want to be ready if they come after you."

"And you're thinking he may be getting close?"

"More than likely."

"Do I need to move again?"

"Don't worry, I'll get him. I mean we'll get him. But...you need to keep me, as well as Lt. Lavender, informed of anything suspicious."

"Give me your phone number and email address."

"No, we'll stick to the burner phones. I don't trust you guys. I know about the bureau's links to fake news agencies and newspapers." Rich said. "I have your number and I'll call you. Every week I'll call you with a contact number. You know I'm at the bar in the days. You don't need to know anything else."

"Settle down, Rich," Bertoloni said.

"Settle down? He's after me, not you. You can just sit back and wait for him to come after me. Then you grab him and get all the glory." Rich got up. "I'm done." He walked out, slamming the conference room.

A young agent at the elevator looked Rich up and down. "Are you being escorted?"

"Fuck off, I'm leaving." The elevator doors opened and Rich stepped in. The agent stood with his mouth agape. "You getting in?" The doors started to close. "To hell with you then."

Two beefy and heavily armed security officers stood shoulder to shoulder as the elevator doors opened onto the lobby.

"You haven't been playing nice with others, Mr. Rice," said one, a smirk creeping across his square-jawed face.

"What're you going to do about it?"

The other officer gripped Rich by the elbow and less than gently urged him forward.

"We are going to convey you to the entry, accept your visitor's badge, encourage you to sign out, willingly return your property, thank you and say Bye Bye."

"Agent Bertoloni called and said you were upset," the officer added.

"We're used to upset."

Rich bent down and signed out. "Then you ought to understand." He took off the visitors badge and handed it to the officer. "Life has become tough and most confusing."

"Us guys are on your side, Mr. Rice." He returned to Rich his side arm.

The door buzzed, tripping the lock.

"Sure you are," Rich waved. "Later, boys."

"*Adios*, Mr. Rice."

Got to keep movin'...Got to keep movin'

Blues fallin' down like hail...blues fallin' down like hail...

Rich couldn't shake the anger that burned inside. He went back to the bar and worked the day, hardly saying a word to Jorge, Daisy or Tom. Delta and Chicago Blues played over the sound system. Robert Johnson's *Hellhound on my Trail* seemed appropriate on repeat play. He broke another glass washing it in the sink behind the bar. "Shit."

"Boss?"

Rich picked the shards of glass out of the sink and threw them in the garbage.

"Boss?"

Mmmmmm...Blues fallin' down like hail...blues fallin' down like hail.

Rich glanced up. Daisy stood at the bar. He looked and saw Tom serve a whiskey sour and Manhattan to a couple at the bar, then amble over. Wiping his hands on a towel, Jorge watched from the kitchen door.

"Are you all right?" Daisy wanted to know.

And the day keeps on remindin' me...there's a hellhound on my trail

Hellhound on my trail

Hellhound on my trail...

Rich said nothing for a while. Then, with tight lips, exhaled through his nose. "No, I'm not all right."

"Maybe you should take the night off?" Tom said, his eyebrows raised and eyes suggesting.

Carefully, Rich set a dripping glass on the folded towel next to the sink. "Yeah. I think you're right."

"We've got it covered, boss."

"No *problemo, Jefe.*"

Rich nodded and walked to the end of the bar. "If you need me, call."

"You bet."

By the time Rich had reached the dumb waiter, Tom had Led Zeppelin's *Good Times, Bad Times* blasting through the bar.

He climbed the dumb waiter where Roommate greeted him. "Hey, Rooms."

"Rup." The little dog turned round and round. His stub tail wiggled excitedly.

Out back Roomy took a leak, crapped and sniffed around the parking area. The air pressed wet and heavy. Rich looked up at slate colored clouds gathering in the dusky blue night. A storm brewed. He couldn't stop thinking about the meeting with Bertoloni and Lavender. He thought himself a hunted animal cornered--they were coming for him, no matter what.

Roomy ran after the big moths swarming around the lights. If there were good things in his life, Rich could count Roommate, Gisele, and The Ordinary. Maybe he only counted the sure things. The rest? Unknown.

He had little appetite, not like Roommate, who loudly crunched his dinner. "I don't know where you put it for such a little guy." They sat on the couch and let the TV churn. A red banner crept across the bottom of the screen warning of severe thunderstorms and possible tornadoes to the north. "A good night for it," Rich thought.

No way could he sleep this night. He got up, fetched his shotgun and Glock and sat facing the window. Darkness enveloped the living room.

Chapter 3

The beat and hum of music and conversation from the bar downstairs echoed in the dark apartment. A thunderstorm lit the midnight blue of the far western horizon.

Rich sat in the straight back chair facing the window. A shotgun lay across his knees.

"I'm the bait," he muttered. "Well, this bait bites back."

Car headlights flashed squares of light on the ceiling, racing left to right, reeling back right to left. The light seemed to run from itself.

Roommate lay on a pillow next to the chair, gently snoring.

Lightning flared and the room burst into quick white light and dancing shadows, flickering about Rich's body.

He waited.

Distant thunder rumbled, approaching.

Rich watched.

Vinton Street between 17th and 16th settled in for a wet night. People dashed, splashing through puddles on the sidewalk, seeking shelter from the approaching storm.

A siren pulsed down 16th street. The Fire Department ambulance swerved onto Vinton. Rich followed the red lights as they lit up the buildings on either side of the street.

The ambulance reminded him of the day he was shot. Arriving for work at the Park Forest Daily, Rich parked. He stepped out of his car then remembered his shoulder bag. As he bent, reaching into the car, fire ripped down his side. He collapsed to the pavement. As he fell he thought he heard a distant pop from atop the construction site across the street. Blood gushed from his side, back and ran down his leg soaking into his jeans. People from the Daily ran out to him.

"Are you okay?"

"I don't know?" Rich said. "I was getting my bag and then I felt burning."

"Call 911."

"Rich, it's Bill More. Look at me. Look at me." Bill kneeled next to him. "Are you all right?"

"What's all this blood?"

"I don't know. Does anyone know what happened? Was he hit by a car?"

"I thought I heard a gunshot," someone said from the gathering crowd.

"Did anyone call 911?"

"Yeah, they're on their way."

"Stay down, Rich. I think someone took a shot at you?"

"Oh, Christ, Bill." Rich swayed against the side of his car. "They're shooting at me now?"

"You might be right, buddy."

"Jesus, I'm really bleeding."

"Someone grab towels. We need to put a compress on the wound."

"Bill...call Gisele, okay?"

"Will do."

In the emergency room, a doctor and nurse cleaned up Rich. The bullet didn't pass through the body, but tore along his side, from his right shoulder blade to his belly. It kissed every rib on his right side on its way out. He sat on the examining table realizing had he not bent forward reaching in for his bag the bullet would've gone through his chest or head.

Gisele rushed in, her eyes wide in panic and mouth open. "Are you okay, baby?" She wore a blue striped jacket and skirt, with white silk blouse, having come straight from the brokerage office.

"I'm fine," he nodded, carefully lifting his right arm. Behind him, a doctor busily sewed red flaps of flesh together.

She stared into his face a long time, caressing his cheek with her hand. "What happened?"

"A lot more than phone calls and slashed tires."

"It certainly is," said a husky man in a yellow windbreaker, striding into the room. Gisele and Rich turned to him. "I'm Detective Jim Dedmon, attached to Chicago PD. How're you doing Mr. Rice?" He talked while vigorously chewing gum. A fidgety sort, with hands in his pockets, Dedmon jiggled his keys and rocked on his heels as if spoiling for a fight. His hair seemed a little too long for a cop.

"Why are you here?"

"A call came in to the office from Bill More, your boss. I took it. I'm glad your wife is also here."

"How do you know Bill?"

"I don't know him. A guy in my office knows him from back in the day Bill worked the cops beat."

"Can I see ID?"

"Here you go." Dedmon pulled out his wallet and shield, flipping it open for Rich. "Knock yourself out." He chewed.

"What did you want to talk about?"

Dedmon pocketed his badge. He searched the room for a chair, grabbing an orange plastic molded one from the corner. He spun the chair, straddling it and crossing his arms on the chair back. Looking down and grimacing, Dedmon started: "I want to talk about saving your life." He glanced over to Gisele. "Maybe I should say saving your lives."

"Richie, what's he talking about?"

"Go on."

"You two have to make some quick decisions--not tonight, not tomorrow, but today and right now."

"Those articles you wrote exposing the Decker's sex ring were great. We got that sick son of a bitch off the street. But...his Russian Mafia friends, the Bratva, were implicated. They don't care for publicity all that much."

"So the calls at 3 in the morning, the keying of my car and Gisele's car, tires slashed and vandalism to my house were not Decker's people, but the Russians?"

"Yup," Dedmon raised his head. "And since that didn't stop you from writing articles about their activity in human trafficking and prostitution downtown and in the suburbs..."

"They tried to kill me."

"Yup again. You about done, Doc?"

The doctor stood up. "Yes, just going to put on a bandage to dress the wound."

"Maybe you can come back and do that."

"Oh, okay." The doctor moved to the door. "I'll be back in a few minutes."

"Thanks, Doc."

"Decker's people are garden variety nasty little pervs." Dedmon explained. "Your articles exposing their rape parties with underage chicks just stopped them from getting laid. You exposed the Russians sex slave operation and that cost them hundreds of thousands of dollars. Face it...they want you dead." His lower jaw rolled round and round, working the wad of gum in his mouth.

"Any idea who took the shot?"

"What? Other than Bratva? No, not really. There are scores of ex-KGB or Russian military in the Bratva. There's good money for the thugs."

"As I was falling I thought I heard the shot from a construction site up the street."

"You did. We went to the top of the building. Didn't find a shell casing. But footprints and some drag marks from a sawhorse indicated someone was up there. And it's right in the sight line for the Daily's parking lot."

"How do you know all this?"

"This is kind of what I do," Dedmon quietly said. "I'm attached to a department in the Chicago Police. Mostly, I liaise with the FBI, CIA, Scotland Yard and Interpol tracking the human traffickers."

"What're we going to do?" Gisele whispered to Rich.

"You're going to disappear." Dedmon had overheard her. "I'm going to talk to Bill and my contacts at the Tribune. They're going to write that you were shot, in critical condition and not expected to recover. I hate to be the bearer of bad news, but you're going to die. Meanwhile..." Dedmon paused. "Mrs. Rice...you also have to disappear and not with your husband."

"I don't want to leave, Rich."

"Listen to him Gisele. He's making sense."

"Can't we get into the Witness Protection Program?"

"You're not really witnesses." Dedmon shrugged. "Besides, that program is bullshit. Too many people know about it."

"He's right, Gis." Rich put his left hand on her shoulder. She shuddered. He looked hard into her eyes. She couldn't return his gaze. "Go up to your mother's in Glencoe. You can still work from home. She'll be okay in Glencoe?"

Dedmon's phone beeped. He tugged it from his pocket. "Yeah...they took a shot at you, not her. This is Dedmon...."

"But I want to be with you."

"It won't be for long. Will it, detective?"

Dedmon took the phone off his ear. "What?"

"We won't be apart for long."

"No guarantees. Maybe a year...or as long as it takes to find the shooter and deport the bastard. They start losing key people they'll back off." He put the phone back on his ear and talked in a low voice.

The doctor stepped through the door and stopped. "Sorry, I thought you were done. I was going to finish dressing the wound."

Dedmon stood. "It's okay Doc. You can finish." He walked over to Gisele and Rich. "That was the FBI. They will protect you as much as they can wherever you head to. And you, Mrs. Rice."

"Baby." Rich rubbed her back with his good hand, smoothing her trembling. "We'll be okay. Listen. Get the long box from the closet. You know—my dad's rifle and automatic."

Dedmon held his hand out and led Gisele to the door. "There's a uniform waiting outside. Tell him to follow you to your house in Park Forest. He'll wait while you pack the essentials for you and for him." They stopped outside the room. An officer appeared. "You don't have kids, right?"

"We had a cat. Someone killed it. We found it on the doorstep in the morning."

"Sorry about the cat. Lock down the house like you're going on vacation and head to your mother's in Glencoe. Stay there." Dedmon reached into pocket. "Here's my card. Call me if anything suspicious happens." He patted Gisele lightly between the shoulder blades.

"Wait. I want to say goodbye to Rich." Gisele tried to turn back. Dedmon twisted her around. He leaned close to her ear. "You'll see him later. I'm going to take him to you. I promise."

Gisele seemed in a daze. "Okay."

Dedmon went back into the emergency room.

"I'll be done with him in a minute," the doctor said.

"Take your time, Doc," Dedmon went to the window.

Rich grimaced as the doctor dressed and taped the wound. "C'mon Doc, gently."

"Can you get me a lab coat?" Dedmon asked, looking out the window.

"Sure," the doctor replied. "I'm just about done."

After the doctor left, Dedmon talked over his shoulder to Rich. "I'm sure they're watching the hospital. You put on a lab coat and go out the back door. I'll pick you up there."

"Thanks for handling Gisele. She took it better from you than she would have from me."

"I've been divorced a couple of times. I'm pretty good at driving women away."

"You going to take me to get my car at the Daily?"

Dedmon sighed. "Mr. Rice...Rich. Remember what I said? You're in critical condition. I'm going to drive you to your mother-in-law's place in Glencoe. You can lay low there with your wife for a day or two. But then you got to take off and get some miles between you and Chicago. No bullshit."

The doctor returned with a lab coat.

"Thanks Doc," Dedmon said. "And Doc...hush hush, okay?"

"No worries. I've got enough shit in my life. Never saw you."

"Thanks for everything, Doc," Rich, using his left hand, shook the doctor's hand.

"Try not to make any sudden twisting movements. You'll tear out the stitches. And remember to change that dressing in a couple of days. It'll drain, so don't be alarmed if it's pus and blood. Those stitches will have to come out in a week or ten days. You can go to any clinic or hospital...or, you can do it yourself. Just douse it with antiseptic after." The doctor reached into his pocket and pulled out a brown plastic bottle. "These are for pain. Take one every four hours."

"What is it?"

"Vicodin. I'm assuming you can take it. I can get you some Oxy, if you'd rather. And sorry, it's going to be an ugly scar."

"No, this is fine." Rich slipped on the shreds of his bloody shirt and tugged the lab coat up his stiff arm. "No problem, Doc. I heard that chicks dig scars."

"Okay, you head down to the side exit at the end of the hall and wait for me. I'll come around with my car. Here put these glasses on."

"Thanks, Detective." Rich took the glasses and carefully walked down the hall while Dedmon went out the front entrance.

They didn't talk much on the long drive up 294 North through the congested western suburbs of Chicago. Rich stared out the window, dwelling on getting shot and nearly killed and what to do next.

Sports Talk radio babbled beneath the hum of the engine and whoosh of the Tollway traffic. Sully and some former pro ball player debated the annual quarterback problems of the Bears. Riding in the new Tahoe, Rich noticed it didn't have a new car smell. In fact, smelled like muddy boots and cheap perfume.

"This a department vehicle?"

Dedmon twitched, chuckled and ground his gum between his canine teeth. "Hell no."

Three rows of cream colored leather seats were set up.

"Family car?"

He laughed. "You're a nosy reporter, aren't ya?"

The litter on the second row of seats consisted of Haribo Ladrillos wrappers, a pair of hot pink ear buds and celebrity magazines in a language Rich thought might be Turkish.

"How many kids you got?"

"None. I ain't married." Dedmon's jaw worked hard. He shot Rich a quick shifty glance.

"You know what you wrote," Dedmon looked back to the road. "About the Russians...it got to them."

"Yeah?"

"They're like cockroaches hiding in a dark basement, scooting along the walls, crawling through the holes and in your kitchen eating your food. Your articles turned the light on in their kitchen." Dedmon laughed. "Oh, they didn't like that. They started to lose money. And we started to see'em in the light. We busted house after house, finding these pitiful young girls. They couldn't speak a word of English. Most were kidnapped from Eastern Europe and some new ones from the Middle East. We deported them back to their homes and families."

"Funny," Rich muttered. "This whole mess started with a guy who lost his wife and a slimy old man and his son who gang raped young girls."

"Not just the girls," Dedmon grinned. "They led us to the pimps. We found the slave owners. We busted a bunch of those roaches."

Rich took out the pill bottle and shook a speckled white capsule into his palm.

"What're you taking?"

"It's the Vicodin Doc gave me for the pain."

"You in pain?"

"I'm starting to feel it. Hurts to take a deep breath."

"Got any extras?" He stopped chewing his gum.

"No. I might need them."

"You got to admire them Russians, though," Dedmon started up again as they continued driving north. "Especially those KGB guys."

"Why?"

"Remember when the Iranian students took over the US embassy in Tehran? They had lots of American hostages."

Rich grunted.

"Well them students also took over the Soviet embassy and nabbed some Russians hostages. So..." Dedmon chuckled. "So the KGB grabs twice the number of Iranian students. They killed'em, then cut off their genitals, stuffed their genitals in their mouths. Then they sent the bodies back to the Iranian students." He slaps his knee, gleefully. "Those Iranians let the Soviet hostages go immediately." Dedmon snapped his fingers. "The garden with the 71 virgins ain't much fun if your dick's cut off."

Interstate 294 merged onto 94 North.

"Yeah...I've heard that story. Not so sure it's true."

"True or not, you gotta admire the KGB for that."

"I need to call my wife."

"You can't," Dedmon cautioned. "You're in critical condition. These guys can check on your calls."

Rich exhaled through his nose.

"So...any idea where you might hide out?"

"Yeah," Rich said. "I figure I'll stay with Gisele in Glencoe until my stitches come out...then I'll head west."

"How far west?"

"My dad was in the Air Force. When I was in grade school we moved around a lot in the west."

"You got relatives?"

"I have a sister in Oregon."

"Out west is not a bad area to lay low for a while." Dedmon said. "I know the Bratva don't have a big presence there. It's kind of disputed territory with the Mexican gangs."

"I'll look for a place with lots of Czech, German and Poles. They don't get along that well with Russians."

"They would stick out like sore thumbs."

"You got any contacts?"

"As a matter of fact, I do." Dedmon fished a small notebook out of his shirt pocket. It had a small pen attached. He flipped it to Rich. "Here, write down this name. Paul Bertoloni. He's an agent with the divisional office of the FBI in Omaha. I don't have his phone number, but once I get back to the station I'll give him a call. When you pass through Omaha call the FBI office. He'll be expecting to hear from you."

"Anybody else?"

"Naw. I used to know a couple of vice cops with Kansas City PD, but I'm pretty sure they retired. You thinking of the Omaha or KC area?"

"Not sure. What's your connection with Omaha?"

"Did a couple of jobs out there recently."

"Yeah? What?"

"Nothing much. Delivered merchandise for a Turkish company."

"Doesn't sound like cop work." Rich tore off the page from the notebook and handed it back to Dedmon.

"Shhh, don't tell my boss." Dedmon smiled and chewed.

The crowded western suburbs gave way to open spaces, wooded acreage and smaller, more upscale North Shore villages and towns as they exited 94 and headed north on Highway 41 at Wilmette. Nearing Winnetka Dedmon let Rich call Gisele. She talked excitedly knowing Rich was on the way.

"Those were a great series of articles you wrote. And..." Dedmon started. "And I was wondering how you got your information."

"At first it was just old man Decker and the people around him."

"Yeah, damn politicians. But what about the Bratva connections?"

"That started with Decker, also."

Rich went quiet. Dedmon's questions made him uncomfortable.

"Yeah, so, it started with the old guy—but how'd you get those guys to talk?"

"You talk to one guy." Rich glanced at Dedmon. "He leads you to another guy...who leads you to another guy. You just have to make the calls."

"I got that...yeah, got that. But there must've been one guy in Bratva that fed you information." The muscles in Dedmon's jaw bounced as he worked his gum.

"One guy?" Rich's suspicions grew. "Not really."

"A couple guys then?"

"Not always."

"You remember their names?"

No way Rich would answer Dedmon's question and reveal his sources. "I can't recall. I'd have to check my notes."

"Where are your notes?"

"At the office."

"The Daily?"

"Exit on Tower Road and head toward the lake," he told Dedmon.

"What? Oh, okay." Dedmon slowed and turned. "Wow...this is some real estate up here."

"Take a left on Green Bay Road," Rich pointed.

"Don't know if I can do that."

"What?"

"Lifelong, diehard Bears fan. I can't be seen going down Green Bay Road."

"Ow...don't make me laugh."

Rich directed Dedmon onto Sheridan Road and into the circular blacktop drive of a heavily wooded property. The square three story house dated from the thirties and was surrounded by a large veranda with a wooden swing.

"Call me before you head out west."

"Will do." Rich groaned, slowly opening the car door. "Thanks, Detective."

Gisele burst out the front door and ran down the steps. "All right, buddy. You take care, okay?

The rain let up. Lightning and thunder passed to the east. Roommate snoozed. Rich sat staring into the darkness, waiting on the dawn. He lived yet another day.

Chapter 4

Bam...Bam--thumped on the metal door.

Startled from a doze, Rich sat upright in the chair. He reached for his .45. The automatic tumbled off the table. It's going to go off, he thought and covered his head.

Keys jingled outside, slipping into the lock.

The .45 clunked to the floor. It did not discharge.

His heart raced. He dived for the gun just as the door opened, hitting the end of the chain.

"*Es* housekeeping," a Spanish woman called through the door.

At that moment, Rich realized he was in a motel room in Omaha.

"*Uno hora, por favor,*" he breathlessly shouted.

"*Si, senor.*" The housekeeper closed the door.

Rich fell back, slowly getting his wits and wind. His right side ached. The stitches were removed yesterday. He looked at the automatic. The safety was on and the hammer not cocked. Hell, he didn't even know if it would work. It was his dad's gun and other than the Springfield rifle, the only weapon he had.

"Don't freak out." Rich pounded his fist on his knee.

"I'm a dead man," he mumbled, climbing to his feet. "I've got to slow down the game or I'm done for."

The noisiest town he'd ever been in. It didn't help that he got to Omaha and checked into the motel around midnight after a nine-hour drive from Glencoe. He tossed and turned unable to sleep with trains coming and going, blowing their whistles, trucks and cars roaring along the interstate nearby, whining jets from aircraft flying in low on approach to land, and then, as dawn lit the edges of the sky, birds, fucking birds, waking and chirping incessantly. Mainly, he couldn't stop the fear shaking in his belly.

Pitching the .45 on the rumpled bed Rich went to the bathroom and rinsed cold water on his face. Glancing up, he caught himself in the mirror. "You need to get serious. They tried to kill you...and missed. Not by much." Mentally, he jotted down what he needed to do, including going to the Omaha police department for a gun permit. "Wonder if I have to register dad's old .45?"

He had an appointment with a real estate agent today, to look at commercial property. The idea came from Gisele. She thought they could buy a store or bar so Rich didn't have to go out and get a job. The idea appealed to Rich. His aunt and uncle in Oregon had a small café bar along the Rogue River at Gold Beach. He worked summers busing tables and washing dishes. He couldn't cook for beans though he knew a little bit about running a bar. Gisele also thought buying a small neighborhood taproom would be a great place to hide. Rich couldn't resist joking. "A bar. That's brilliant. Who'd look for a reporter in a bar?"

Still feeling his way around Omaha, Rich found the real estate office on Dodge Street following advice from a convenience store attendant. "Everything in Omaha turns off 72nd and Dodge."

Early for his appointment, but his agent Georgette Cohn had the time. A petite brunette with an animated manner, Georgette did not match the youthful picture on the realty company's web site. Her small face wore a reddish gloss on pale cheeks and ruby red lips parted in a white smile. They met in a side conference room.

"Aren't you warm in that sweatshirt?" Cohn asked, plucking the heavy black sleeve. She wore a bright striped yellow top with white slacks. Her clothes were a shade too eye-catching, tight and perhaps a tad too young for her.

"No," Rich replied, peering down on his black White Sox hoodie. Nervously, he rearranged the front, concealing the .45 in his shoulder holster.

"I have two commercial properties that fit the requirements you sent me." Cohn arranged flyers and slid them over to Rich. The first, a gray two-story building with full parking lot, met Rich's specifics. The photo of a dreary red brick multi-story property appeared on the second flyer. The property looked abandon. Asking price for either property lay within Rich's range.

"This gray property," Georgette pointed to the flyer. "Is located in North Omaha, 30th Avenue, near the start of the Florence area. The second is in South Omaha."

"I would like to see both."

"Of course," the agent picked up the flyers.

"I'll drive," Rich volunteered.

"You don't have to."

"I'd rather. I'm still finding my way around and you can help me."

Cohn gathered her phone, property folder and oversized black bag. "Be glad to. Are you parked out front?"

Rich rose. "Yes."

"Let me tell my assistant I am showing properties and then we can go."

They walked out of the real estate office with Georgette making small talk, asking Rich questions. Rich grew uncomfortable answering.

"You're moving from Chicago?"

"Chicago area...suburbs."

"I only know you as Rich. Your last name is?"

"You don't need to know that. I'm acting on behalf of someone else."

"Can I ask who?"

"Miss G. Esslin."

"Is that your wife?"

"I'm divorced."

"Oh, sorry to hear that," Georgette said with an expression that was anything but.

"Thanks." Rich clicked open the doors to his truck.

The agent hesitated at the side door. She looked at the climb to the passenger seat with mouth agape. "You know I can drive. My car is just over there."

He saw her predicament and said, "I'd like to drive, if that's all right."

Cohn hefted her bag, phone and folder onto the seat and clutching the door armrest, grappled up to the seat. She almost fell out reaching for the door to close it.

Rich saw it all and pinched his nose to disguise his amusement. "Okay. You just tell me where to go."

Breathless, Cohn said, "take Dodge east to 480 and then north."

They drove down Dodge Street with Georgette pointing out areas of interest. "This is the University of Nebraska-Omaha and a very nice area if you were house hunting." Rich nodded. "And this is Memorial Park. Every

Fourth of July they hold a concert and top it off with a spectacular fireworks display. That whole hillside is filled with people."

Rich murmured: "Uh huh."

The agent's tone changed when they merged onto 480 North.

"This area is North Omaha and I'm not sure you're going to like it."

"Why's that?"

"It's the part of Omaha we call," Cohn hesitated. "Well, it's known as Dark Omaha."

Rich shot her a glance, wearing a blank expression on his face. "What does that mean?" He knew without asking.

Her eyes darted left and right. "There's quite a lot of...a lot of...um...coloreds."

"I don't care for that."

"I know," Cohn added. "It's so difficult to sell in that part of the city."

Rich grunted and let it go. "I'm trying to set up a business. My consideration is purely toward making the business successful. So what kind of neighborhood is the second property located in?

"That's in South Omaha. It's primarily Mexican, but with white Irish, Czechs and Bohunks. That's the funny name they call themselves."

"Sure they do."

At Ames Street, driving north Rich saw what Georgette was referring to. Large groups of blacks gathered at the corner and in a McDonald's parking lot. The agent squirmed in her seat.

"Are we close to the property?" Rich asked.

"No...about five more blocks."

A series of brownstone and brick buildings, the campus of Metro Community College spread out to the left.

"It's actually the site of Fort Omaha, a historic landmark." Cohn said. "Keep going straight here. This is the outskirts of Florence."

"Not Omaha?"

"No, it's still Omaha—but a hundred years ago it was annexed by Omaha. This was almost the capitol of Nebraska and not Lincoln."

"Really." Rich glanced around. Florence was a mix of architecture from the twenties through the forties. There were few modern design homes.

"The property is up there, next block," Georgette motioned. "On the left."

"Gotcha." Rich came to a stop at a light. A park with rows of houses lay on the right. The neighborhood seemed okay, if not too quiet. "So this is a historic area?"

"Yes, and not just that it almost became the state capitol. The area was the site of Mormons winter camp on their trek to Salt Lake."

"Really?" Rich said. The light changed to green and Rich drove on.

"Up the hill is the Mormon museum...and further down is a bridge over the Missouri River which marks the crossing."

"Okay."

"The property is right there." Cohn pointed out a long gray two-story building. The front of the property had lapped vinyl siding with a small rectangle window and windowless door in a recess. A sign denoted T's Crib in block letters above the doorway and a white banner for the lottery. T's Crib had a fairly large parking area. Rich pulled in and turned off his truck.

"Before we go in, tell me about this place."

Georgette shuffled papers and came up with the flyer. "It says 3,000 square feet, including 1,000 square foot parking area. The downstairs bar is 1,100 square feet, with kitchen and dining area. Annual revenue $150,000 to $250,000."

"That's a fairly wide revenue swing," Rich said, scanning the littered and cracked parking lot. A new two-tone black and cream Lincoln sedan next to an older Ford sedan with dimpled plastic back fender were parked in the back.

"Property taxes, business taxes, license fees estimated $12,000 annual. Whoa, there's a lien on the property in the amount of $20,000."

"That's the owner's problem. And the upstairs living quarters?"

"A two bed, one and a half bath, 900 square foot living quarters upstairs...with separate entrance."

"Kind of small." Rich ducked down and looked up to the upper level. "Okay...what do they want for it?"

"It's listed at $350,000 and says: Seller Motivated."

"Are sellers anything but motivated?"

"Only on foreclosures."

"Good one. Let's see the inside." Rich jumped. He waited while Cohn climbed down.

"Owner's name is Tyrone Johnson," she said as they walked across the lot. "He's owned the property for the last 20 years."

The agent tried the front door. It was locked. She knocked hard with her small fist.

"Where's the separate entrance?"

"Not sure. I called yesterday and said we would be out this morning." Cohn hammered on the door. "He said he'd be here." A series of locks could be heard opening on the other side of the door. "Lazy," she murmured quietly to herself.

"Yeah...yeah," the bolt drew back. "Who dat?"

"It's Georgette Cohn, Mr. Johnson," she talked loudly into the closed door. "I'm the agent that called yesterday and said I would bring out a potential buyer."

Opening the door, a six foot, 300 pound plus older black man yawned and wiped his eyes. His big round belly was barely contained in a red sleeveless Nebraska basketball t-shirt. His gut hung over a pair of shiny white trimmed black track pants. "Oh yeah," he said, scratching his short gray peppered hair. "I 'member you." He stepped back.

Georgette rushed briskly past Tyrone, ignoring him.

Rich went in and looked around. Certainly smelled like a bar with that close stink of stale beer, peanuts, well used cooking oil, cigar smoke and people. Empty now and dark, Rich could make out a side room with pool tables, a kitchen area and picnic tables covered in red checked plastic, scattered square tables and mismatched short bar on the other side. In the rear was a green felt poker table littered with overflowing ashtrays, stray poker chips, empty glasses and bottles. Sports memorabilia and pictures of black entertainers dressed the walls.

With eyebrows raised, Tyrone watched the real estate agent dart about.

Rich turned, with his hand out. "Tyrone? Nice to meet you. My name's Rich."

"Likewise, Rich." A smile split Tyrone's big face. The two shook hands. "I meant to clean, but it was a late one last night." He had a slow southern drawl.

"No problem. I understand."

They ambled around as Rich surveyed the bar. Cohn stood in the middle with manila folders clutched to her chest. He noted state lottery and Sportsman's Park race results posted on a white board behind the bar, next to another display of numbers.

"Is that a jukebox?"

"Sure as shit is."

"You don't see too many Rock-Olas around these days."

"It don't make me no money."

"Can we see upstairs?" Georgette asked.

Tyrone stopped. "I'm sorry. My wife and her mother are upstairs sleeping. I ain't going to wake'em"

"Understood," Rich said. "It's a two-bedroom, one and half bath."

"Yep."

"Up-to-date kitchen?"

"Pretty much, new appliances a couple of years ago. They'll stay."

"Basement?"

"Half basement for inventory and storage."

"If you don't mind me asking, Tyrone," Rich wondered aloud. "Why are you selling?"

"Well," Tyrone sighed, sitting on a bar stool, resting a fat forearm on the bar. "My wife, she's got the cancer. Her mother's up from Mississippi. She's only got maybe half a year left and wants to go back to Mississippi to be with her family."

"Sorry to hear that." Rich said.

Tyrone looked at Cohn. She said nothing.

"Yeah, thanks," he replied. "I've had this place for about twenty years. Raised a family upstairs and put kids through school and..." he trailed off.

"Seen enough?" Georgette asked Rich.

Rich paused. "Yeah," he said, holding out his hand. "Thanks, Tyrone. Best of luck to you and your wife."

"Aw right. I'm here if you got any questions."

Rich waved, trailing the agent who was halfway across the parking lot.

"Like it?" she asked as Rich started up his truck.

"Bet he makes money hand over fist."

"Didn't look very lucrative to me."

"He probably has regulars that have been going there for most of his twenty years. But that's not how he makes his real money."

"Not following you...take a right up here."

"Did you see the Sportsman's Park track results behind the bar? It's a little betting parlor. Those numbers on the board? He's running his own numbers racket."

"How much can you make doing that?"

"Not as much as you can make running an afterhours, high stakes poker game. Probably charged each guy hundred bucks to get in the game, and he got maybe ten percent of each pot."

"You want to make an offer then?"

"No. His regulars won't come if I buy the place. And you said the Florence area is Mormon. They don't drink or gamble."

"Well...let's check out the second one." Cohn said. "Take Highway 75 south."

Rich adjusted the .45 tucked in the shoulder holster under his arm and beneath his sweatshirt. The weight and shape comforted him.

"I don't know Omaha yet," Rich asked. "I wonder if you know the best place to buy some protection."

Georgette shot Rich a look of horror. "W-w-well, you can go to any drugstore."

"What?" Rich screwed up his face. Then he got it. "No..." And he chuckled. "I meant a gun or shotgun."

The real estate agent appeared relieved.

Rich rocked with quiet amusement as he drove down the highway. "That...is the first good laugh I've had in weeks."

"Glad I made you laugh," the agent wiggled in her seat. "I don't really know a lot about that. My boyfriend does. He goes to Cabela's or Luna's pawn shop. There are also gun shows."

"Okay. Thanks."

Making quick hand signals, Georgette motioned Rich to exit Highway 75 at L Street. "And take a left at the light."

"So what's the story of this part of Omaha?"

"This area was the northernmost border of old South Omaha, a prosperous and separate area called Packing Town after all the meat packing plants. It was all feedlots, banks and processing plants. Immigrants flocked to the area to work, Irish, Czech, Italian, German and Eastern Europeans." Georgette read from a flyer. "Omaha gobbled up Packing Town as large cities do. Now it's known as South O or South Omaha. Most of the packing plants were gone by the end of the sixties and now the area's notoriety is largely due to its concentration of Hispanics. Turn left at 24th," she added quickly.

A colorful neighborhood and noticing the mix of people, Rich liked the area right away. In part because it suited his needs to disappear into a community. They traveled up 24th Street. He drove by the generations with architecture from red brick and pillar Romanesque buildings to fifties modern with angled walls to sharp corners.

"Cinco de Mayo and going out for a Mexican dinner are really fun down here," Cohn absentminded added. "Take a right on Vinton Street."

The street and side streets were a mismatch of thirties row houses, fifties ranch homes with wrought iron columns and modern tri-levels. The sight of old brick streets branching off Vinton fascinated Rich. The crescent turn of Vinton reminded Rich of streets in cities in Europe.

"Interesting area."

""It's right up here," Georgette said, pointing to a dirty brick two-story triangular building on the corner. "Turn left on 16th and then park."

Slowly, Rich turned while checking out the building. He eased to the curb and switched off the ignition.

The building seemed to have been vacant for quite some time. A tattered and sun bleached To Lease or Buy sign lay crooked in a corner of the display window. A Mattress Omaha Outlet sign over the doorway belied its past and last failed enterprise.

Rich flipped open the glove box and took out a flashlight. He got out and circled around to the passenger side. Georgette struggled to find her footing on the running board. "Here, let me help you." Rich reached, taking her arm and helping her down.

"Thank you."

"No problem."

They stood on the corner and surveyed the building.

"When was it built?"

The agent opened a folder. "1935," she replied. "During the height of South Omaha's meat packing era. Ummm, rebuilt, including foundation, in the late sixties.

That's when it was remodeled into a tavern and..." she paused.

Rich turned. "And?"

Georgette sighed. "And the upstairs was a...hostel."

"Hostel? Like a youth hostel?"

She glanced away. "Well..."

Rich chuckled. "You mean there were lots of beds upstairs."

"Yes,"

"Now I am very intrigued to see the insides of this place."

Georgette fished around her large bag as she walked to the back of the building. "I have the code for the lockbox on the rear gate."

Rich followed, slowly, squinting in the noonday sun, looking the building up and down.

A seven-foot chain link fence, topped by tangles of rusted barbwire, surrounded a weedy overgrown gravel parking area in the back. Rich noticed a corner of the chain link had been cut and pulled back, enough to crawl through. The agent opened the lockbox and pulled out a ring of three keys. She picked through the keys and found the one matching the big lock hung on a length of chain wound between posts at the gate. Rich stood behind her and surveyed the gravel lot. It appeared large with space to accommodate three or four cars and maybe a dumpster. A long flight of iron stairs climbed the side to a small grated landing and back entrance to the second floor. The stairs had a hinged section in the middle with a cable to a corroded pulley on the roof. At one time, the stairs could be raised preventing access to the second floor. That appealed to Rich. New cables could be installed. That was a plus in his evaluation of the building. Double doors allowed entry to the first floor, with a concrete well and steps to the basement adjacent.

Georgette struggled with the lock on the chain.

"Here," Rich stepped forward. "Let me do that." He unwound the heavy chain from the poles. The gate swayed and squeaked as he pushed it open.

"You have basement delivery and storage. Then main and upstairs, um, living quarters."

"Are there keys to the basement?"

"Yes."

"Let's start there and I can check out the foundation, electrical and plumbing."

They walked to the stairwell and stopped.

"Oh my god," the agent gasped.

A bent, beat up shopping cart, wadded newspapers, plastic bags and bottles, food wrappers and other garbage heaped the stairwell. A rectangle cut of old, oily black plywood lay across three steps from the bottom corner. A frayed blue tarp held in place by broken bricks covered the front.

"Be it ever so humble," Rich said. "How long has the building been vacant?"

Georgette checked the flyer. "More than eighteen months...almost two years."

Rich carefully picked his way down the concrete steps, kicking aside debris. With flashlight in his hand, he tore off the blue tarp and hit the light. Piles of newspapers and empty cans of chili and beans were strewn about a frayed moldy green sleeping bag. A rank odor came up from the corner. Rich reeled back, his hand over his nose and mouth. The stink traveled up the stairs.

The agent squealed. "What is that smell?" She pulled a tissue from her purse and held to her nose.

""It's okay," Rich clicked off his flashlight and reached up for Georgette. "It's not a dead body. That's one good thing. You got the key?"

The agent took Rich's hand and cautiously placed a foot down each step.

"Oh, it smells horrible."

"Key?"

"Here." Georgette handed Rich the key.

He slipped the brass key in the lock. Stiff and frozen, Rich twisted the key hard before the bolt clanked open. He turned the knob and set his shoulder to the stuck door.

"Is the electricity on?"

"I don't think so."

Inside, the basement was dank and smelled rank. Shafts of light from street level half windows lit small areas of the basement. Dust, like snowflakes, drifted through the light. Rich played the beam of light over the room. He felt the agent come up close behind.

"Do you think there are any rats?"

"Stay here, by the door and let me poke around...okay?"

Rich slipped his hand under the sweatshirt and on the butt of the .45. The illuminated white circle drifted over the large basement, showing a pile of mattresses in plastic in the middle of the room, boxes and furniture, and not much else. Rich put the light on the furnace in the corner, then followed ductwork, electric lines and plumbing in the rafters. He shined the light on a circuit box on the wall by the door. The wiring looked fairly modern. He stepped over a dusty roll of rug and put light on a wood rack in the middle of the basement. Silver tubes dangled from the ceiling above. This is what Rich hoped to find. These were keg tubes to the main floor. The wood frame was for kegs and gas canisters. On closer inspection the tubes were cracked and needed replacing, but at least the structure was there.

Something scratched and scuttled along a far wall. Rich chased it with the beam of light.

"Not funny," the agent said at the door.

Rich didn't reply. Storage room and shelves were in the far corner of the basement. He panned the light across the foundation and saw no cracks nor water-stains. He'd seen enough.

"That was really creepy," Georgette said as she quickly went up the steps.

"Yeah, it was." Rich agreed, locking the basement door.

"So what are they asking?"

Looking at the flyer, the agent replied, "$450,000."

Rich opened the back door and snorted at the price. "This is a foreclosure, right?"

"Yes.

"And it's the land as well as the building?"

"Yes."

"Okay," Rich muttered, as he entered a backroom and storage area. "It's been vacant almost two years. How long was it on the market?"

"Three years. The bank foreclosed a little over a year ago."

They went into a kitchen area, with stainless steel counters, shelves and open half window to the main room. There were wells with 240 volt electric outlets. Rich turned the faucet on a sink. The pipes knocked, but water came out. "This needs a fryer, griddle, stove, refrigerator and freezer."

"Doesn't seem like too much."

"That's a chunk of change that'll come off the four fifty."

From the kitchen to the main room, Rich nodded seeing a long bar made from thick dark mahogany running the length of the wall. Pillows and bedding, with SALE signs were scattered atop the bar and a couple desks. The floors were red oak and appeared in good shape though dirty. He went behind the bar.

"This'll need taps, new sinks and an ice unit." He ducked out from under the bar, looking in a side room. "A pool table there." And turning said "A stage over there."

"There's a dumb waiter back here, with a ladder," the agent called out. "Oh, now what is that smell?"

"Formaldehyde."

"Formaldehyde? Like a funeral parlor? I thought this place was a mattress and bedding store."

"They spray used mattresses with Formaldehyde to kill the bugs. I venture they weren't selling only new mattresses. And that shit causes cancer. The seller is going to have to get rid of'em."

Rich walked to the bathrooms, opened the doors and checked the Ladies and then the Gents. The gents had a cracked urinal and the ladies needed stall doors. The tiling and sinks were in passable condition. He followed the agent out the back door.

"What do you think?"

"So far?" Rich replied. "You heard me thinking out loud on what equipment I'll need. That's not even taking into account what upgrades will be needed to the plumbing, electrical and roof." They started up the stairs to the second floor. "To answer your question...not bad."

They paused at the top of the iron stairs. "We got a view," Rich said.

"These are rickety stairs," the agent said, clutching the handrail. "Can I have the keys?"

"Sure."

Georgette sorted through the keys, trying one that was wrong.

"Try that one. We haven't used it yet."

The door opened and the agent stepped in. "Wow."

"Wow? Now what?" Rich followed. He saw immediately what had impressed the agent. A smallish kitchen gave way to the large open area with hardwood flooring, high ceilings and windows along the 16th Street side. Divided by a wall the living room was quite spacious. The upstairs was stuffy, but didn't have any of the bad odors like downstairs. The doorway to a bedroom lay at the far end of the room. A good-sized bedroom with windows overlooking Vinton Street had a doorway leading to a master bath with shower. The bath décor reminded Rich of the thirties. Small black and white tiles and a pedestal sink, with a toilet and box completing the vintage Italian restaurant appearance. Another door lead into a laundry room, with hookups for washer and dryer. Then they were back in the kitchen. Lacking only appliances, the kitchen seemed in good condition with a granite top center island and stainless steel sink and well for refrigerator and stove. "Not like any whore house I've ever seen."

Leaning into the pantry Georgette said, "Here's the dumb waiter from downstairs. The ladder looks like it goes up to the roof."

"Good," Rich replied. "I want to check the roof." He went into the pantry and stepped onto the ladder. "It's a little tight." He climbed through the dark and stopped near the top. Hooking a ladder rung in his elbow, he pulled out the flashlight. There was a trap door with a latch. Holding the light in his mouth, Rich pulled back the latch. A crack of sunlight shone through. Carefully, the trap door creaked as he pushed it open and climbed onto the flat tar and gravel roof. Pocketing the flashlight Rich walked around inspecting the roof. It appeared recently tarred, with a fresh coat of gravel. He hadn't seen any water stains on the ceiling downstairs so knew the roof water tight. That was another plus.

"You okay up there?"

He checked the rooftop A/C unit, ventilators and exhaust pipes. They were free of birds nest or other obstructions. At the front of the roof he scanned Vinton Street up and down. He liked this building, but $450,000-- no way.

"I'm coming down."

"How was the roof?" Georgette had her purse and folder on the center island in the kitchen.

"It's in decent shape."

"This upstairs is quite a nice surprise." She paused. "So...now what do you think?"

Rich looked around, nodding. "I've more pluses than minuses. You know...I think I like it."

"You've locked in financing?"

"I have a backer...I'm paying cash."

"Oh...that might reduce the price a bit."

"It's listed at $450,000?"

"That's comparable to other commercial properties in the area."

"That may be, but it's going to cost me around $70,000 to $80,000 for repairs and to get this place fitted with appliances and equipment, not to mention inspections, insurance, licenses and fees."

"Well, what do you want to offer?"

"$325.000," Rich said.

"I don't think they'll take that."

"Probably not. And it's not what I'm willing to pay. The building's been vacant for two years. Do you know how many others have looked at it and passed, or had their financing fallen through?"

"I think you should offer $375,000. They would counter with $425,000 and then you'd meet in the middle at $400,000. That's $50,000 less than asking."

Rich, scowling and with one eye closed, silently regarded her a moment, wondering if she worked for him or her commission. "No. I am willing to pay between $350,000 and $400,000."

"Then why not offer $375,000 right now?

"It will be worth that once I make the improvements. You know it doesn't work that way."

"Maybe I should speak with Miss Esslin."

Rich turned on her, angry. "No. If you call or email Miss Esslin we will drop you and your company. Understand? Everything goes through me. Got it?"

"Okay," the agent said, her hand up. "Let's go back to my office and write up an offer."

Driving back Georgette made another pitch for Rich to raise his initial offer. He'd lose the building she thought. Rich stayed firm in his initial offer of $325,000.

A week after they had tendered the offer, the bank countered with $400,000. That told Rich they would take less, much less. He came back with $340,000 ignoring Georgette's further protests. Another week went by. Then the bank threatened to tear up the offer. Rich knew they wanted to sell the building, and quick. So he told Georgette to come back with $350,000 and mention they were looking at a similar property in Florence. The next day the bank agreed to $350,000. Georgette had neglected to tell the bank it would be a cash transaction and they would not get the financing. The bank tried to back out, but they had already accepted the offer and Rich held them to it.

"Gis," Rich said over the phone. "We got it."

"That's great, Richie. Did they agree to the price?"

"Yup. I beat'em up real good, babe. You'd be proud of me."

"I already am. You know this is nearly all our retirement savings."

"I know. But I think while I'm hiding out I can get this place up and running and then, when everything blows over and we can be back together, we can turn it over for a good profit."

"I know we can. You have to be a fool or in a bad economy to lose money on real estate."

"True."

"I miss you so much. Is there any way we can see each other?"

"I miss you too. Maybe in a couple of weeks we can meet someplace like Des Moines, just for the weekend."

"Never thought of Des Moines as a romantic place, but it'll be as romantic as Hawaii if we can be together." Gisele laughed, a short, sad laugh. "Are you safe? Anything more from the Russian guys?"

"Yes, I'm safe. No—nothing. I'm pretty sure they still think I'm dead. But I worry about you sweetheart. Be careful, okay?"

"I will. I'll shoot you an email on Telegram under the Keeper name with the details of the money transfer. I love you."

Chapter 5

Keys in hand, a thick bundle of papers and manila folders tucked under his arm, Rich hustled from the Title Company office to his truck. He could barely contain his excitement driving to his new property.

Once the building inspector had signed off the sale closed within two weeks. Rich kept busy getting his bartenders license, applying for state and city liquor licenses, filling out forms for various permits and contacting vendors for everything from carbonics, to linens, popcorn and peanuts. Water, gas and electric were turned on and a dumpster was scheduled to be dropped off that afternoon. Signage presented a minor problem.

"I want the sign to be...The Ordinary," Rich explained to the middle-aged man leaning on the counter, filling out a work request.

"Okay...ordinary what?"

"Just...The Ordinary."

"An ordinary font?"

"The Ordinary, but in Olde English."

"I'm not following you, sir. He scratched the back of his neck with a yellow pencil. "You want an ordinary sign in Olde English?"

"Yeah," Rich replied slowly. "I don't understand why you're not getting what I'm saying." They looked at each other a moment. "Here...let me have a sheet of paper." He plucked the chewed pencil from the other man's hand.

His head turned sideways as he watched Rich do a rough sketch. "Oh, it's called The Ordinary."

Rich took care of the most important permit, the conceal/carry gun permit. He bought a used Smith & Wesson .38 and practiced almost daily at an indoor range. Yet, even wearing a side arm he didn't feel completely secure.

Unlocking the gate, he drove into the gravel parking area. All of his belongings were in a knapsack, a long box and cardboard carton. He'd fled the Chicago area with little more than the clothes on his back and what Gisele had grabbed when she got out of Park Forest for Glencoe. Shouldering his knapsack, taking the boxes, Rich checked to see if the hole in the corner of the chain link fence had been repaired. It had. And the pile of garbage in the stairwell to the basement had also been cleaned up.

Opening the door to the second story flat, Rich dropped his belongings on the kitchen island. He tore the plastic packaging off a new mobile phone and plugged it in to charge. Rich went around and unlocked a window, letting in fresh air and a gentle breeze. He left the other windows shut.

He surveyed the flat. "I need a sleeping bag and I bet I could find a mattress in the basement."

The dumpster was off-loaded in the afternoon and Rich set to work filling it. He dragged a new mattress up to the flat and let it flop in the middle of the living room floor. While in the basement, he again heard something scrambling along the walls. "I might need to get an exterminator in," he quietly said to himself. Clearing and cleaning gave him a momentary reprieve from his constant vigilance.

Dusk took him by surprise. He hadn't even put a dent in the cleanup, but he had to call it a day. He closed the window, locked up and went out for food and bedding. Darkness had descended by the time he got back. He locked the gate behind and carried white bags of Chinese take-out and a new sleeping bag from Wal-Mart up the iron stairs to the second story. He wearily reached the landing. It had been a long day.

Inside he opened the long box and pulled out the .45 and tucked it in his back pocket, taking the inside holster .38 revolver and laying it on the mattress. He went up the dumb waiter to the rooftop with a couple of cold beers and his dinner.

The colorful lights of Vinton Street's taqueria, hamburger joint, café and package store glowed between streetlights. Cars moved up and down, in motion like the couples and groups walking on the sidewalk. Rich settled in the shadows of the raised edge at the front of the roof, eating, sipping beer and idly watching nightlife on the street.

The months since the shooting had taken a toll on Rich. Laying low, always on guard, ever suspicious and using false names had drained him. Yet, sleep eluded him. He slept like a man in combat, in short fits and snatches. And never a deep sleep. The slightest sound, a crack or thwack, would see him wide awake and straining his ears to hear what approached in the darkness.

And now all the guns. Rich had not been a gun nut. Not that he was anti-gun. His dad taught him firearm safety and how to shoot. At camp he loved the smell of cordite and putting a good pattern on target. "Ready on the right. Ready on the left. Ready on the firing line. Load one round of ball ammunition." He'd plink at black targets twenty yards away. Rich learned to handle a weapon with respect. Especially when a kid down the line shot the tip of his ear off looking down the barrel of a loaded rifle. The only weapons in Rich's house were his dad's Springfield rifle and the vintage .45 automatic, army souvenirs. Since Rich's father's passing they had stayed in the closet.

The sniper changed all that. He constantly wore the .45 in a shoulder holster or had it close at hand. If he didn't have the automatic near him, he would get anxious. The change in his attitude became apparent one night at Gisele's mother's house in Glencoe within days of the sniper's attempt on his life. Rich woke with a start, hearing a noise downstairs and certain someone was trying to break in. Where was his .45? He searched the dark bedroom, becoming more and more frantic. Gisele woke, sleepily asking: "What're you looking for?" The gun. My gun. He threw clothing all over and jerked out all the dresser drawers. "It's in the long box in the closet...where you put it." With the .45 in his hand he calmed down. Peeking out the door he saw Gisele's mother climbing the stairs with a midnight snack of milk and cookies.

He often thought that he would rather not be carrying a gun. But he knew that until the threat from the Russian Mafia was gone, he couldn't be too careful.

Too much food. He tossed the spoon in the carton and set it aside. Looking at the night and the lights of South Omaha, Rich wondered if he and Gisele could ever be together again. She was sort of safe, staying with her mother in Glencoe. The Russians probably knew she was there. They would leave her alone thinking they had shot and killed Rich. If they ever thought different, it would be the first place they would go. He didn't want to think about that.

In Glencoe she could continue working her brokerage accounts, which she was exceptionally good at. Gisele was the package, smart, tall with athletic good looks, knew the market and worked hard for her clients. And her clients were loyal, not just because she made them money. The adage: you don't invest in the brokerage, you invest in the broker, was true regarding Gisele.

The false names, cheap "burner" phones, blind emails using a dark web browser were the subterfuge ensuring Rich didn't turn up on the internet. Not an easy task with the pervasive social media and search engines.

A midnight breeze out of the west put a chill to the air. Rich gathered up his bottles and cartons, tucked in the .45 and climbed down the dumb waiter. He latched the trap door securely. Half-light lit the flat from a single lamp on the floor of the living room by the mattress. He tossed the empties and food cartons in a waste can and put the rest on the kitchen island. Rich locked the back door and gave it a shake. It rattled. He angled a chair under the knob, then kicked it tight on the floor. It would do. Weariness came over him. He was ready to hit the mattress. No guarantee he would get to sleep, though perhaps if he lay down for a while.

"Gisele, it's me. Everything okay?" Rich clicked on the safety and set the .45 by the mattress. The phone to his ear, he lay back on propped pillows.

"Yeah," she slowly replied. "It's late and...I'm lonely for you."

"I'm lonely for you also. Are you still at your mother's?"

"Yes."

"Gisele...it's not safe. You need to get another place. If they come looking for you the first place they'll go is your mother's."

"Rich." Her voice sounded impatient. "You know I can't. Mom had that seizure last year and since dad's passing she's been battling depression. I can't leave her alone."

"I just worry about you. Promise me you'll get out of there soon?"

Gisele ignored the question.

A train whistle sounded in the distance--two short blasts then a long wail.

"Is that a train?"

"You can hear that?"

"Yeah. Is it close?"

"Not real close. I think it's the westbound California Zephyr. I hear trains coming and going all the time."

"Hey, do you have a cousin in New York?"

"Not to my knowledge...why?"

"I got letter from some guy in Brighton Beach claiming he was your cousin and wanting to know if you left a will."

Rich made a disgusted noise deep in the back of his throat. "Sounds like a scam."

"No doubt. I have to deal with these people. They're like vultures."

"Sorry, Gis."

"I get letters and calls from lawyers offering to represent me in a civil suit against whoever tried to kill you."

"Lawyers. Tell them to fuck off."

"I did." Gisele paused. "Richie, I hate all the lies. People wish me sympathy and condolences. I picked up five new clients this week because they think I'm a widow and feel sorry for me. How long is this going to go on?"

"I don't know, Gis. I just don't know."

"Did you call the FBI?"

"I've been busy. I have to get the bar open."

"Promise me you'll call tomorrow."

"I will…"

"No, promise me," she insisted.

"I promise I'll call the FBI if you promise to look for another place." Rich's response met with silence. He sighed. "Listen, Gis. I need Tom Waller's phone number. You have my book can you look it up and email to Keeper?"

"Tom? Why do you want that guy's number?"

"Tom's a good bartender. We did a lot of gigs when we were at college. He's just a little rough around the edges."

"Rough around the edges?" Gisele scoffed. "Tom Waller is rough in the middle all the way out to his ragged edges. You think he'll come to Omaha?"

"I can only ask. I've got to go. Miss you."

"Richie, I miss you so much."

"Love you, Gisele." Rich clicked off the phone, lay his head down and let his eyes close.

A crash, clang and the sound of a glass bottle rolling across the kitchen floor woke Rich. He snatched the .45, snapped off the safety and scrambled to his feet. Barefoot, dressed only in his briefs, Rich crept to the kitchen. Gun up, he leaned in, taking a quick look. The waste can lay on its side, with wads of paper and food containers strewn about. The beer bottle slowly rolled to a stop at the back door. Rich didn't see anyone. He stepped into the kitchen. Then something black with patches of white, about the size of a large rat, darted from behind the island to the pantry.

"Holy crap," Rich whispered. "That's a big damn rat." He cocked the .45.

At the pantry doorway he heard a low growl coming from a shadowy corner.

"Rrrrrrrrrrrrrrrrrrrrrrrrrrrrrrrrrrrrrrrrrrrrrrr..."

"Never heard a rat make a noise like that. What the hell are you?"

Rich switched on the ceiling light.

There in the corner shivered a bone skinny black and white Boston terrier. Turned sideways, his back hair up, the dog paced. "Rrrrrrrrrrrrrrrrrrr..." In other spots hair lay in oily mats, with patches of skin and red inflamed areas showing. Its eyes and nose were all but crusted over with some kind of black and yellow gunk.

"Well, well," Rich eased down the hammer of the .45 and squatted in the doorway. "What's up, lil fellow?"

A torn food carton with teeth marks lay in the opposite corner. The terrier's bug eyes anxiously jumped from Rich to the container and back.

A length of thick gray galvanized wire was wound tight around the animal's neck. The wire had worn raw the flesh of the dog's neck and the twisted sharp ends under its chin cut long bloody and pus gashes under its chin. Rich inched closer. The terrier moved away.

"What's on your neck? Is that a collar?

"Rrrrrrrrrrrrrrrrrrr..." The growl came with less threat.

"Let's make friends." Rich stood and went back into the kitchen. He laid the .45 on the counter and picked up the waste can, bottles and papers. "I think I have something for you to eat." He had half a carton of fried rice left and poured out half on a paper plate. He tore down the sides of another carton, rinsed it out and filled it with water. The little dog peeked around the door of the pantry. It backpedaled to the corner when Rich returned with the plate and water.

"Here you go." He set the food and water down.

The terrier sniffed, taking tentative steps toward the plate.

"I've got some wire cutters. I'll be right back." He could hear the dog eating the rice behind.

When he returned the dog jumped and scrambled back into the corner. "Rup...Grrrrr..." Rich reached down and grabbed the squirming dog. "Sorry, kid. I have to do this." Pulling the wire up from the open flesh made the dog kick and squeal. He snipped the wire and let the dog loose. He turned the wire over in his hand. It was covered with dried blood and black hair. The terrier shook its head and scratched its neck. Curious, it set his buggy eyes on Rich.

"Who put this on you? I'd like to put one on them." Rich tossed the wire on the counter and wet a cloth under warm water.

The dog had finished the rice and lapped at the water. Rich came closer. Freeing him from the wire around his neck let the dog know Rich meant no harm. He wiped the crust out of the dog's eyes and nose, then dabbed at the oozing cuts under the chin and neck.

"Seems like I've got a roommate." The small dog gazed up at Rich, its big brown eyes plaintive. "Was that you hiding in the basement?" The dog sneezed, licking its lips.

"Okay, Roommate. I'm going back to bed. It's the Vet for you tomorrow. We need to have those wounds treated and see if you have a chip."

Rich shook out the rest of the fried rice and refilled the water. Yawning, he retrieved the .45 and shuffled back into the living room, falling on the mattress. A few minutes later Rich felt the little dog cautiously step onto the mattress. "Settle down, Roomy," Rich murmured sleepily. Circling, then curling between Rich's legs, the terrier took a deep breath and sighed.

Itching ankles woke Rich an hour later. "We are definitely seeing the Vet tomorrow."

The next morning, "Denny Feldstein"--the name popped in Rich's head as he opened his eyes awake. He wondered for a moment, reaching down to scratch his leg, jostling the sleeping dog at the foot of the mattress. Then he realized what it meant. Last year Rich wrote a news piece on Denny Feldstein, a mid-level Chicago area drug dealer. Denny had a dog with a rare medical condition, and Denny loved his doggie. With the cops after him, Denny took off. The Feds notified veterinarians across the country. Sure enough, a Vet in Arizona got a visit from Feldstein and his ailing dog. The Vet called the Feds and Feldstein was apprehended.

"Sorry, Roommate."

Rich could not risk exposing himself by taking the dog to a Vet. He scratched the top of Roommate's round head. The sleepy dog blinked open his eyes and stretched.

"I can get over the counter shampoo to rid you of those bugs. Then I'll clean the wounds on your neck. Don't worry, Rooms, I'll take care of you."

Rich rose and picked the .45 from the floor by the mattress. He dressed. Roommate followed him around, watching, wondering.

"I'll be back with food," he told the terrier. He kicked away the chair bracing the back door. Roommate started to whimper.

When Rich returned, he filled the kitchen sink with warm water. Roommate devoured the dish of dog food. Just as the dog finished Rich raised him up and slowly lowered him into the water. Roommate struggled, glancing back at Rich with fear in his eyes.

"Easy, Roomy. Everything is fine." Rich squeezed out flea and tick shampoo on Roommate's back and scrubbed it into a lather. The dog settled down and let Rich wash him. Carefully, he cleaned around the dog's neck and the open cuts. He could already see the wounds closing up. Drying him off, Roommate shook and snorted. "Looking a helluva lot better, Rooms," Rich said, putting the dog back on the floor. He shook and skidded sideways, then licked his paws.

The slip of paper Dedmon had given him with the name of an FBI agent was in his knapsack. He went back into the kitchen and leaning on the island, dialed the phone number on his burner phone.

"FBI, may I help you?"

"Hello. Could you connect me to Agent Paul Bertoloni."

"Certainly. May I say who's calling?"

"Richard Rice."

"Is he expecting your call?"

"I think so."

"I'll connect you. Please hold."

The line went silent.

"Paul Bertoloni."

"Agent, my name is Richard Rice," he started. "I was given your name by Jim Dedmon from Chicago. He said to call you once I was in Omaha."

"I know Dedmon and I recall him sending me an email to expect a call. That was about a month ago. Why haven't you called?"

"I don't know. I just didn't do it."

"From what he wrote me of your case that was a pretty reckless thing to do."

"Maybe so."

"So you got my number from Dedmon. What do you know about him?"

"Not a whole lot. I met him at the hospital after I was shot."

"Was that the only time?"

'Yeah. Why?"

"No reason," the agent replied. "I've got some notes up on my computer about your case. Give me a minute to review."

"Sure. Take your time."

"Okay. That's too bad about your editor."

"Excuse me? My editor? You mean Bill More at the Daily?"

"Yeah."

"What about him?"

"You didn't know?"

"Know what?"

"Bill More was killed about two weeks ago."

"Oh, God. Killed. After I left?"

"Says here it was a burglary gone bad. Apparently, late at night, he surprised some intruders at the Daily office. They slit his throat."

"Slit his throat?"

"Yeah. You know that's unusual for burglars. Usually, they just take off running."

"What'd they take?"

"Not much. They turned over some desks. Yours being one of them. And snagged some computers. Again...yours."

"Did they catch them?"

"Not yet, nope." Bertoloni paused. "You know the Russian characters after you aren't punk amateurs. We need to talk. I can go where you are or you can come here."

"Why don't you come here."

"Where are you?"

"Vinton at 16th. I'm working in a red brick building—turning it into a bar."

"All right, Mr. Rice. I'll come by this week or next and we'll talk. Listen, if something comes up or if Dedmon contacts you--call me.

Chapter 6

Steadying himself on the top step of a rickety wooden ladder, Rich pushed coaxial cable through a hole in the ceiling in the back room of the bar. He'd mounted surveillance cameras outside the front, back and side of The Ordinary. The cable came up in the pantry of the upstairs flat. There he had set up a router and computer. Roommate sat at the base of the ladder, his head cocked aside, watching.

In the bar room Mose Alison's piano jazz played low. "Talking 'bout your woman...I wish you could see mine. Talking 'bout your woman...I wish you could see mine." Rich softly sang along. "Every time she starts to shakin' she brings eyesight to the blind."

Something outside the bar got the small dog's attention.

"Once I get this cable rigged to the computer upstairs," Rich breathlessly explained. "Then we'll see how the cameras work. Then we..."

"Rup...Rup." Roommate dashed toward the front door, yapping in alarm.

Rich clamored down the ladder and slipped on his flannel shirt to conceal the .45 in the shoulder holster he wore.

"Rup...Rup."

"What's up, Rooms?"

The terrier barked at the front door, turning round and round.

Halfway to the door Rich could make out a shadow in the tinted glass. He stopped, reaching for the .45 under his left armpit.

Tink...tink...tink, metal, like a key, tapped at the glass.

"Rup...Rup."

"Who is it?" Rich yelled.

"Omaha Gas," a voice loudly replied. "I've got a couple of gas canisters to drop off for..." the voice paused.

"Rup...Rup."

"...for The Ordinary bar."

"Easy, Roomy. It's okay." Rich patted and scratched the little dog. "Good boy." He slid the steel bar aside and twisted the latch unlocking the front door. Sunlight flooded the entrance alcove as Rich pulled the door open. Roommate went to the open door, but was blocked by Rich's foot.

"Rup...Rrrrrrrrrrrrrup..."

Out on the sidewalk a short black man in faded green overalls looked down at a clipboard and asked. "Are you Mr. Keeper?"

"I am," Rich said. "That should be delivered in the back." The dog peeked around Rich's leg.

"The gate was locked."

"Okay, I'll meet you at the back gate."

"Truck's on 16th street."

Rich closed and latched the door and slipped the bar across. "Roomy, you stay here." He crossed the bar to the dumb waiter. "I'll be right back." He slid down the ladder and came out in the dark basement. The basement was clean, organized with newly constructed wooden racks for kegs and CO2 canisters. He flipped a wall switch and four low watt bare bulbs in the ceiling lit the basement. Rich unlocked the basement door and mounted the steps. The cement stairwell was also clean, bleached and hosed down.

The gas truck's brakes squealed, stopping at the gate.

Opening the lock and pulling the heavy chain through, Rich walked the chain link fence back as the truck slowly drove in, parking behind Rich's black pickup. The driver hopped down and went to the back while pulling on a pair of well-worn leather work gloves.

"I used to deliver here six or seven years ago," he said, jumping up onto the lift gate.

"Oh yeah."

"Yeah." The driver wrestled one, then a second gas cylinder. "It was a bar before it closed. They made it a bed store..." He rolled the cylinders onto a handcart on the lift gate. "That tanked too." He lowered the lift gate. "Now you're making it a bar again?"

"That's right."

"Good luck."

"Thanks." Rich pointed. "You can take those down stairs."

"I remember."

Rich hung back as the driver wrestled the handcart down the stairs and into the basement.

"Where you want these?"

"There," Rich pointed.

A floor above, though muffled, Roommate could be heard barking.

"Big bark for a little dog," the driver said, unloading a cylinder from the handcart.

"The heart of a Rottweiler."

"Wouldn't want to cross him." The driver twisted the second cylinder off the handcart. He brought out a clipboard and made notations. "I'll need you to sign for the delivery."

Rich scribbled *Keeper* on the signature line and handed back the clip board. The driver tore off a sheet and handed it to Rich.

"Thanks. When do you think you'll open?"

"Two, three weeks, maybe."

"Good luck."

"Tell you what. Come by for a beer on the house."

"Thanks. I will."

"Great. See you then." Rich followed him out and up the stairs. He watched as the driver turned the truck around and drove out. He pushed the gate closed and looped the chain around the bars, clicking the pad lock. He returned the driver's wave as he roared off. Walking back to lock up the basement, Rich's phone beeped.

"This is Keeper."

"*Senor* Keeper?" a heavily accented Spanish voice asked. "You advertise for cook?"

"Yes."

"I interview?"

"Sure. How about this afternoon?"

"This I can do."

"You know where we are?"

"*Si* I...no...I don't...where?"

"The red brick building on Vinton at 16th."

"I be there. What time?"

"About one or two. And your name is...?"

"Is Jorge. Jorge Ruiz."

"All right, Jorge. I will see you about one or two this afternoon. Bring your resume, references and be ready to cook something."

"Oh, I be ready. *Gracias, Senor* Keeper."

"Okay...good-bye."

Roommate met Rich as he climbed up the dumb waiter ladder to the bar room level. The terrier sniffed him all over. Rich chuckled and scratched the little dog. "Do I smell like the basement?" he asked. "Let's finish the cabling for the surveillance eyes."

Back up the ladder, Rich worked the cables, while Roommate sat below the lowest rung, watching curiously.

Rich spent the remainder of the morning and much of the afternoon running coaxial cable and hooking up the router and computers upstairs and under the bar. Once connected, he clicked on the surveillance cameras. With a flicker, all four camera images flashed on the computer screen. He stooped and squinted. Number three camera on the 16th street side needed adjusting. But the back view camera, door and Vinton Street cameras were aimed correctly. Rich ducked under the bar.

"Where are you Rooms?"

The terrier snoozed on a folded blanket in the side room.

"Come on, pup."

Roomy woke with a jump.

With an eight-foot folding ladder in one hand, Rich unlocked the front door with the other.

"*Senor* Keeper?"

Startled, Rich swung around. A Hispanic man walked toward him. Roommate stopped at Rich's feet.

"Yes?" Rich brought the ladder around from the side, holding it in front him like a shield.

"I, Jorge, the cook. You see me today?"

Jorge wore his black wavy hair long and combed back. He stood maybe five foot five, losing an inch or two from the bow in his legs. Dressed in a long sleeved striped shirt that needed the attention of an iron, black jeans and pointed cowboy boots, he stopped before Rich and held out his hand. Rich noticed tattoos. Jorge grinned from an uneven row of yellowish teeth. Rich rearranged the ladder from one hand to the other and shook Jorge's hand.

"Let's go inside. We can talk." Rich noticed Roomy sniffing Jorge's boots.

"Dis your dog?"

"Yeah."

"What's his *nombre*?"

"Roommate."

Jorge squatted and scratched under Roommate's chin. "Hey, *poco hombre*." The dog huffed with his tongue out, blinking at Jorge. Rich took notice of Roomy's reaction to Jorge.

"Come on, Roomy." Rich propped the ladder against the bar. "Have a seat at the table."

"*Gracias*." Jorge stopped just inside the bar. "*Senor* Keeper?"

"What is it?" Rich sat at the table. Roomy came up to Rich's feet.

Jorge stood awkwardly, sideways, his head down. It struck Rich he looked as if he was ready to leave. "I have to ask, *Senor* Keeper."

"Ask away."

"Do you hire...felons?"

Rich studied Jorge for a long moment. The question didn't surprise him. The other man gazed down and away, unable to meet Rich's eyes.

"I go," Jorge suddenly said, taking a step toward the door. "I sorry I take your time."

"Hey," Rich snapped. "I haven't answered yet."

"But I know..."

"Jorge," Rich added firmly. "Sit down. Let's interview for the job before I answer your question."

"Okay, *Senor* Keeper." Sheepish, not fully understanding, Jorge slowly took a seat across from Rich.

"And drop the *Senor*, Keeper will do. Want some coffee, water, soda?"

"*Gracias*, I fine."

"Did you bring your resume?"

"I no have resume. I don't know what it is."

"A resume is a record of where you worked the last five years."

"Oh. I work at taqueria and café and Nogales Mexican Restaurant."

"As a cook?"

"No, kitchen work and cook help. Last two years I cook."

"Where was that? A hotel? Restaurant?"

"A kitchen in...in, ah...in Lincoln." Jorge dropped his head.

"Was that the state pen?"

"*Si.*"

Rich sighed. "Well, okay. Let's put it all out on the table. What were you in for?"

"I steal car."

"Two years for stealing a car?"

"It not the first car I steal."

"Why'd you steal it...joy ride?"

"No, I need money."

"How long have you been out?"

"Nine months."

"Where you been working?"

"Nobody hire me."

"How you been getting by?"

"My wife. She work."

"What does she do?"

"She clean houses."

"Cleans houses? You know, I'll need a cleaning crew for this place."

"Sure, you no hire me. You hire her."

"Jorge," Rich paused, shaking his head. "Relax. We're still talking."

"Yeah. We talk. It do no good," Jorge sounded resigned.

"Why are you working so hard to make sure I don't hire you?"

"I no do that."

"No? Your tone of voice. Your comments that I'm not going to hire you. Your whole..." Rich made circling motions with his hands. "Your whole body language. You act like it's a foregone conclusion I'm not going to hire you."

"That the way it been," Jorge shrugged. "...especially since you be..." He stopped himself.

"...since I'm white?"

"You say it, not me."

Rich ignored Jorge's comment. "You graduated high school?"

"*Si*, right here. South Omaha."

"You raised around here?"

"I born in Compton, California."

"How'd you get out here?"

"Papi, he come to work in packing plant."

"How'd you get to be a cook?"

"I good at math in school. I great being cook. I always cook with *mi madre* and work in restaurants helping cooks when little."

"What kind of restaurants?"

"Mex, course. But I also work white, I mean American restaurant. All kinds." Enthusiasm raised the timbre of Jorge's voice. "One time...one time I work at restaurant and cook...he like mescal...he pass out, and I do whole dinner shift...one handed."

"Single handed. That's pretty cool."

"Yeah, *si*. Then they give me *Lunas*, Monday night. Cook not happy."

"What happened?"

"Cook, he start hitting me. He hit me when nobody look. Then I have enough. I hit back. They see. They fire me."

"Doesn't sound fair."

"It not."

"That's when you started to steal cars?"

"No, I work here...there. Then my wife, she get pregnant. I need money."

"So, you have one kid?"

"No, I got three now. They my beautiful angels." He grinned.

"What're their names?"

"Isabel, she 13. She oldest. Frida. She smartest. Jorgelina, *mi bamba* and *mucho* pretty."

Rich noted how Jorge's face lit up. He could tell he loved his daughters very much. "So what's your biggest frustration?"

"*que?* What?"

"Frustration. What disappoints you about yourself?"

"Oh...I know. I not man in *mi casa.*"

Rich stared at Jorge a long time, thoughtful. Jorge squirmed in his seat. "Come with me." Rich got up and Jorge followed into the kitchen. "I've got all the appliances in, griddle, fryer, cooktop, refrigerator and microwave. And there's counter space and cutting boards."

Jorge walked past Rich. "It look good."

"I've got hamburger and cheese in the fridge. Buns, pickles and all that. Can you make me a cheeseburger?"

Jorge took an apron off a hook and tied it around his waist. "How you want it cooked," he said smiling.

"Medium well."

"You want works?"

"Not this time. Just plain."

"Got bacon. I make *muy bueno* bacon, cheeseburger."

"No," Rich grinned. "But I like your thinking."

"Toast bun?"

"Yeah."

Jorge poked through the plastic packages of hamburger buns. "You got plain buns."

"That's all."

"You know what good? A sourdough bread bacon cheeseburger. Keeper, I make best." Jorge went to the sink and washed his hands. "Gloves?"

"There's a new box up there." Rich pointed.

Jorge opened the box and took out a pair of clear plastic gloves. He opened the refrigerator and took out a package of hamburger patties. He leaned down and turned on the griddle. "You got seasonings?"

"Just salt and pepper."

Rich left Jorge to cook. Roommate came up snorting, shaking, yawning and licking his lips. Rich took a box of dry dog food from a cabinet and filled a small bowl on the floor. The terrier trotted up and started eating.

"Jorge?" Rich returned the dog food to the cabinet. "I've got some work to do outside. Let me know when the burger is ready."

"No worry, little *hombre*, he watch. I sing out."

Rich turned, then leaned back in through the doorway. "And think about what kind of menu you could put together."

Dave Brubeck's *Take Five* played on the sound system as Rich fetched the ladder and went outside to adjust the surveillance camera. Afternoon sun warmed his shoulders and face as he squinted looking up at the camera. The heat didn't bother Rich, it was the mid-summer humidity that drained him of energy. Rich climbed up, loosened the mounting bolts and aimed the camera eye to look down 16th Street.

"*Senor* Keeper?"

"Yeah?" Rich tightened the mounts and tried to wiggle the camera. It didn't move.

"Your burger. She ready."

"Thanks, Jorge. Be right in."

A plate and glass were set on the table, with a folded napkin on the right side. The burger smelled delicious. Roomy, with both paws on the chair, his head bobbing as he sniffed the air, agreed.

"Hey, Rooms. This is my lunch." Rich shooed away the terrier and sat. He picked up the burger and did a quick inspection. The patty was evenly cooked, the bun toasted and cheese melted. As a burger, it looked good. Rich took a bite and chewed. The middle of the burger was light gray and just slightly pink, cooked medium well, per Rich's request.

Jorge wiped his hands on a towel, then untied and hung up the apron. "Is okay?"

"Mmmmmmm," Rich replied, mouth full and nodding. "Is great. Come on and sit. Tell me your ideas for a menu."

"Glad you like burger."

Rich pinched off a small portion of the burger and fed Roommate. "Hamburgers will be the mainstay, but what else would you put on the menu?"

"I do full dinner."

"No," Rich interrupted. "No fancy entrees. Bar food, snacks, pub grub they call it."

"*Si*, burgers, fries, tacos, burritos, nachos, quesadillas, *sopas*, salad. I can get enchiladas from Jacoby's." Jorge thought for a moment. "I do scratch pizza."

"Really?"

"Little Italian queen in jail, she teach me to make dough, sauce and all. I make great Mex pizza with chorizo, peppers, *queso—mucho gusto*."

Chewing, talking while he went over to the bar, Rich reached into a folder under the bar. "I think you're a good cook and I like your menu." He came back to the table with papers in hand. "I need you to fill out this application. You are eligible to work?"

"I have social security card. You hire me?" Surprise lifted Jorge's voice.

"Yes, Jorge. I'm hiring you."

A smile broke across his face. "*Gracias*. Thank you, *Senor* Keeper."

"Just call me Keeper...remember?"

"*Si, si*, I remember. I very happy."

"I'll pay you $12 an hour to start. After six months we can talk about an increase."

"*Muchos gracias.*"

"The hours will be hard."

"You no worry. I work hard."

"I know that, Jorge. I meant hard hours. You'll have split days—10 in the morning until 2 for lunch. And 4 until 8 at night. Will that work for you?"

"*Si.*"

"You'll have Monday and Tuesday off, not Saturday or Sunday. Can you handle that?"

"I handle it. I go Sunday mass at 9."

"Later on I plan to hire a second cook, part time. But right now you're the man."

"Is fine. I don't know what to say. *Gracias.*" Jorge started choking up.

"I do need you to go down and take a drug test. Will that be a problem?"

"No, *Senor* Keeper." Jorge was emphatic. "I no use."

"If I did a background check would I have any other surprises?"

"No. I promise."

Rich left a bite of hamburger on his plate and set it down for Roommate. "I've got stuff to do around here. You finish filling out the application." He stood. "You start this Saturday at 10. We've got to get the kitchen set up. I want to open in a couple of weeks." He held out his hand.

Jorge took Rich's hand in both of his and shook it. "I thank you much."

"Welcome aboard." Rich extricated his hand from Jorge's grasp. "And have your wife come on Saturday. I would like to meet her. And I may want to hire her to do the cleaning."

"She be happy. My angels be *mucho* happy." Jorge bent forward, filling out the application.

Roommate loudly worked his pink tongue around the plate.

Rich stooped under the bar, checking the computer and camera on 16th Street.

Saturday morning on the upstairs pantry computer, Rich noticed something suspicious on the front door surveillance camera. A bundle of rags lay heaped in the corner of the doorway. He put down his coffee and checked the clip in his .45.

"Come on, Rooms. We've got to check something downstairs."

With Roommate tucked under his arm, Rich climbed down the ladder in the dumb waiter. He set the dog down and Roomy immediately started sniffing around.

Quietly, Rich eased the iron bar out and unlocked the latch on the front door. He stepped out. Up close the pile didn't look like rags, but like someone huddled in a hooded sweatshirt with a duffle bag at its knees. Rich poked at a leg with the toe of his right shoe.

"Get up, buddy. You can't sleep here."

The mound stirred and groaned. "Dammit, Richie. I was just dreaming about Gisele."

Rich recognized the voice. "Tom? When the hell did you get in?"

"About five. I took the late bus out of Denver."

"You should've knocked."

"I did." Tom yawned. "I figured you weren't here. What's the idea of the gun?"

"I guess I didn't hear you." Rich glanced at the .45 in his hand. "It's a long story."

"Not sure I want to hear it."

"It's pretty boring. Hey, I need you to do something for me."

"Anything, Rich."

"Don't ever call me Rich. Okay?"

"Sure," Tom sounded confused. "You want me to call you Mr. Rice?"

"Not that either. Just call me Keeper."

"Keeper? How'd you get that name?"

"My mother. She used to tease me and say I was a Keeper."

"Paging Dr. Freud. Okay...Keeper."

"Same old Tom." Rich reached down to help him up.

"Seriously," Tom said as he struggled up. "Last I heard you were nominated for a Pulitzer for news stories exposing a bunch of Russian sex traffickers."

"Therein lies the tale." Rich held the door open for Tom.

In the early morning light, Tom appeared aged, but largely unchanged from college days. Rich realized this was wishful thinking for his old friend. Tom moved a bit slower and more stooped. Deep lines ran down his face and wrinkles fanned out from his eyes. The look in his brown eyes seemed weary, yet retained a hint of brightness. His head shone shaved and shiny. His beard had grown longer and though streaked with gray, looked good cut square at his chest. Tom's eyes darted about devilishly as he inspected the work in progress that was The Ordinary.

"This place is a dump."

"Hey," Rich froze and turned. "Remember?" He raised the .45.

"It's still a dump." Tom dropped his duffel bag by a table strewn with sawdust and power tools.

"We're opening in two weeks." Rich holstered the .45 and went into the kitchen.

"Who's this little fellow?" Tom sat.

"I'm making coffee," Rich said. "That's Roommate. He's my guard dog."

"No wonder you're packing." He bent his face low to Roommate. "Hey pup...how you doing?" He pet the terrier gently down its back.

"I've got eggs, bacon, bread and orange... ah no, sorry, I don't have any orange juice."

"Eggs, bacon, toast and coffee would be excellent."

"Over easy?"

"Ha, you didn't forget."

"I've got a cook coming in at 10, but if you're hungry now..."

Tom crossed the bar room to the kitchen door and leaned his shoulder to the jamb. He idly watched Rich cooking on the griddle.

"So...Tom," Rich sounded serious. "What's been going on?"

"Just shit." He said in a hard voice. "Laurie took Jimmy and skedaddled up to Seattle. She said if I didn't get my life sorted out I'd never see her or Jimmy again." Tom had a faraway look in his eye, as if he wished he could go back and do it all over, only this time, not screw it up. Perhaps he had wasted a second chance, and a third and fourth chance as well. "That was a month, maybe two months ago. When I got your call...and I can't believe I was sober enough to answer...I realized Laurie was right. I had to get out of Portland."

"I don't know if I would call you sober when I called." Rich turned the strips of bacon.

"I've been to meetings. I'm a couple of weeks sober."

Rich cracked two eggs and opened them on the griddle. He glanced over to Tom. "A couple of weeks sober is a good start."

"That's partly why I came out, Rich..."

"Keeper!"

"You're going to tell me why Keeper later? I thought coming out here, getting away from the brew scene in Portland and all my drinking buddies and those brew groupies would be a good thing."

"Brew groupies?" Rich shook salt and pepper on the eggs.

"Keeper...you would not believe the gals that hover around the craft brew scene in Portland. Anyway, I thought I could come out here, next to the middle of nowhere, work for you, save my money and go to Seattle to get Laurie and Jimmy back."

"I'll do what I can for you. You can stay here for a while, but I would like you to get your own place."

"No problem. I have a cousin in Bellevue and she said I could stay with her."

Rich pulled a plate from a stack. He slid a spatula under the eggs tipping them onto the plate. He added the bacon on the side, buttered the toast, then handed the plate to Tom. He set out two mugs for coffee.

"Looks good," Tom said. "You may have missed your calling."

"Go on out and I'll bring the coffee." Rich handed Tom a fork and knife.

"So what's all this Keeper shit about?" Tom said as he crossed to the bar room. "And where's Gisele?" He settled at the table and sliced up the eggs. "What happened in Chicago?"

Rich came up with a mug in either hand. He sat, slid a mug over to Tom and then snatched a half piece of toast off Tom's plate. Roomy trotted after. "I'm on the lam, Tom."

"What?" Tom said with his mouthful. "From who?"

"I got an assignment to write about some guys that were connected to the Russian Mafia's sex operations in Chicago. I wrote a series of articles, exposes in the Trib and the cops started busting them. Then, the Bratva, were after me. Me and Gisele were harassed and threatened." He sipped his coffee. "Three months ago someone took a shot at me. I was lucky. I only got wounded. The cops told me I needed to get out of town."

"Is Gisele okay?"

"She's okay. They aren't really after her. They think I'm dead."

"That's why you're Keeper?"

"Pretty much." Rich stared down at his coffee. "I was afraid at first while recovering from being shot. Sudden moves, loud noises, made me jump. You know the sensation when you turn and there's someone right there. You almost leap out of your skin. But at the same instant you're paralyzed and can't move nor think."

He took another drink.

"Then I got angry, real angry, in a rage. Gisele had to physically restrain me. I was going to get those sons of bitches threatening me, threatening my wife, making our life a living hell."

"One morning I woke. Well, I opened my eyes from a short, shallow fit of sleep. I can't sleep anymore, neither deep or long. I woke and wasn't afraid. I wasn't angry either. I had become calm. I knew what I had to do to survive. Oh don't think I embrace the situation—I accepted it and refused to be defeated."

"Whatever you need, you can count on me, Keeper."

"I knew I could." Rich turned the mug in his hands. "I need you to tend bar while I run the place. Gisele and I have sunk our retirement into this deal. We didn't have money for me to just be hiding out for years. So we set up The Ordinary to replenish our retirement and generate the money I need to stay alive. I'm told this will blow over in about a year. Then I can miraculously recover..."

"From being dead?" Tom chuckled aloud. "Nice trick."

"It can happen," Rich smiled.

"And you trust me behind the bar?"

"Yeah, I do. You know how many bartenders I've met who are in the program?"

"A lot, I know."

"You want Laurie and Jimmy back, don't you?"

"I do." Tom gazed down at his plate.

"You want me and Gisele to be safe?"

"Gisele, for sure. That woman deserves a medal for keeping you upright, fed and facing forward. I'm not so sure about you."

"I'll kick your ass if you ever take a drink inside The Ordinary?"

"Yeah, you would." Tom agreed.

"Honestly, Tom. Weeks sober doesn't mean shit. Six months sober, doesn't mean shit. None of it means shit unless you admit you have a problem." Rich dropped the last corner of toast on the floor for Roommate. He swayed forward on his elbows. "One year sober. That means something. Tell you what—I'll give you an extra $100 for every month you earn a chip."

"What if I don't earn a chip?"

"I'll turn you out, brother. Tough love."

"Tough love?" Tom wiped his mouth, grinning. "Wearing that black T-shirt and shoulder holster," he closed an eye and cocked his head, "is that your dad's .45?" He lay back in the chair. "You look like Bullit. Tell me you got a sweet green '68 Mustang outside?"

"I wish." They laughed. "We need to go out to the boonies and do some shooting."

"I love shooting your dad's .45. Remember that World War One sniper rifle he had?"

"The 1903 Springfield...I still got it."

"Cool." Tom clapped his hands together. "We're definitely going out target shooting."

A hard knock sounded on the door. Rich checked the clock over the bar.

"Shit," he hissed. "That's the cook, Jorge and his wife. They don't know squat about any of this...and I don't want them to know. Give me your shirt."

"What?"

"I've got to cover my weapon."

Tom took off his shirt and Rich pulled it on as he walked to the door.

"And remember...it's Keeper...just Keeper."

"Gotcha...and you can call me Ismael."

Chapter 7

"Dammit, Richie, I missed you. It's so good to hear your voice..."

The longing in Gisele's voice spilled out the phone, yet somber by the frustration of their long separation. The months apart wore heavy on Rich as well.

"Miss you, babe." He sighed. "I think there's an opportunity coming up when we can see each other."

"It's been forever."

"Now that The Ordinary is open, we have money coming in."

"I've seen the weekly take in the bank account. It's good." Gisele let Rich maneuver the conversation away from their being apart. "Did the opening go well?"

Rich chuckled. "I put out flyers with coupons for a free burger or hot dog all over Metro Community College and South Omaha. I got a handful of those back. But it wasn't until I set up a Free Beer sign out front did we fill the tables and all the stools along the bar."

"Free beer?" Gisele laughed. "Richie, we have to make money. Don't be giving the store away."

"I know," Rich replied. "I only poured short ones after the first full beer bought."

"Okay."

"It was a better idea than Jorge's."

"Which was?"

"He meant well," Rich started. "He went over the Missouri border and bought a box of fireworks."

"Aren't those illegal?"

"It's a gray area in this town. Yes and no."

"Something happen?"

"No," Rich fibbed, unconvincingly. "Well, yes. Jorge was out front shooting off sky rockets when one sort of...misfired."

"Anyone get hurt?"

"No, no...nothing like that. Instead of going up, the sky rocket went straight down the sidewalk, scattering pedestrians and startling a couple of dogs."

Gisele giggled.

"Then it burst in the street right in front of a police car. I had to go out and play peacemaker between the police and Jorge. That ended the fireworks display."

"Speaking of fireworks," Gisele paused. "Tell me more about seeing each other."

"I've got a plan, Gis. Well, I'm working on one. Probably in a month."

"Well. I've held out this long."

"Me too," Rich agreed. "We have to be careful. Once I get the thing set up, I'll send you the info on Telegram encrypted email."

"I can come out there?"

"Not sure that's a good idea. What if they follow you out of Chicago?"

As if reminded, Gisele asked, "Did you meet with the FBI guy yet?"

"I called him last week and he said he would come down. But I'm not sure when."

"You have to get them to protect you."

"I am well aware of that."

"You promised me..."

"Yeah, yeah," Rich interrupted her. "If I don't see him this week, I'll call him...promise. And did you get another place to stay?"

"Actually, mom's been better. I've spent some time at our house in Park Forest."

"They know those places," Rich mildly protested. "You've got to get something like a studio apartment in Glencoe."

"I will. That creepy Dedmon guy called."

"Dedmon?"

"I don't recall giving him my number. But he called."

"What'd he want?"

"He wanted to know where you were."

"What'd you tell him?"

"I said you were moving around out west. Something bothers me about Dedmon. I can't put my finger on it."

"Good call, Gisele."

"He got upset. Then he got belligerent and started asking questions. I didn't answer. His voice got loud. I wanted to tell him to fuck off, but finally said I didn't know where you were—you were still on the road."

"That's my girl."

"Your girl doesn't like this shit, Rich. Dedmon, this whole thing scares me and pisses me off at the same time."

"Don't trust him."

"You be careful. This crap has changed you. You're not as tough as you pretend." Gisele hesitated. "I'm not that tough either."

"I don't know about that, Gisele."

"How's your roommate?"

Rich leaned over and patted Roommate, curled up on a cushion on the couch. "He's fine. He's snoozing right next to me."

"Tom?"

"No, I thought you meant the dog." Rich smiled. "Actually, Tom moved out to his cousin's house. He said I was charging him too much rent."

"Rent? What were you charging him?"

"Zero."

"Seems like his price. Is he staying sober?"

"So far, he is." Rich knew Gisele neither trusted nor thought very highly of Tom. "He's doing the 12 step. I went to a meeting with him. He's got a temporary sponsor. I told the guy to let me know if he back slides."

"You went to a meeting? Are you...?"

"...drinking too much? No, I haven't fallen to the bottom of a bottle."

"I...I can't say that."

"I can understand."

"The fucking tension..." Gisele had a catch in her voice. "It's unbearable sometimes. I just had to...to be able to sleep."

"I know. I don't sleep well either."

"Mom's worried."

"We'll be okay...this can't go on forever."

"Yes." Gisele's voice shook. Rich wasn't sure if she was on the verge of tears or anger.

"I have to go to work...love you, Gis."

"Love you too. I'm waiting for that email."

Rich checked the mag of his .45, then pushed it into the shoulder holster and walked into the kitchen, standing for a moment watching Jorge dressing three plates of nachos. He spooned on guacamole, sour cream, filled small cups of salsa, all the while rocking his shoulders in time to Los Lonely Boys cover of *Evil Ways* playing in the bar.

Rich smiled and turned to leave.

"*Jefe*, sorry, I dint see you."

"That's cool, Jorge," he waved. "I didn't want to bother you."

St. Louis was batting against San Francisco on the wall mounted TV. The sound was off, but Rich saw the Giants were up by a run in the top of 7th. That meant they were playing at AT&T Park. He'd been there a couple of times and liked the ball park.

Two young couples laughed and talked excitedly as they drank their beers. Three tables had people eating. Daisy, the new waitress, stood at a fourth table taking a food order. Rich checked, and the drinks were already on the table. Daisy was a lucky find, like Jorge. A tall, slim, black girl in her late twenties with a cute floppy rounded natural bob that framed her oval face and accentuated her high cheek bones and big brown eyes, she seemed always in a good mood. Rich knew her disposition disguised the bitterness and hard scrabble of a rootless and parentless childhood. He admired Daisy because of the long hours she worked at The Ordinary while carrying a full class load at UNO. She was going places.

Richie Valens' *La Bamba* bubbled over the sound system.

Five guys sat at the bar, three together and two at the end. Tom had both hands on the bar and was talking to the older man and younger one. Rich ducked under the leaf and stood behind the bar. From habit, he looked to the computer screen, seeing if the outside front and back were clear.

"Hey, Keeper," Tom called with a quick flick of his head. "Come on up here. There's somebody I want you to meet."

"Sure thing." Rich moved up the bar. "How we doing here?" he asked the trio.

"Okay."

"Need a refill?" He pointed to a glass nearly empty set before a middle-aged man in a black and multicolor NASCAR cap.

"In a minute, yeah."

Rich came up to Tom. "What's up?"

"Keeper," Tom held out his hand presenting an elderly man seated next to a much younger man. Same chin, similar nose, the two bore a strong resemblance. "It's my pleasure to introduce you to Virgil and his grandson Stephen."

"How do."

"Nice to meet you," Virgil replied in a thin, croaking voice.

"Same here."

"Virgil, I'm sure Keeper would like to hear you tell him what you did in World War Two."

"Aw, naw, I don't want to bore the guy."

"Come on, grandpa."

"I'll get you two a couple of pulls," Tom slipped past Rich.

"I'd like to hear, Virgil. I'm interested in history."

"Well, okay then." Virgil's long angular face held deep furrows and lines etched in his sunken cheeks. His short, sparse, snow white hair needed a combing over the rounded crown of this head. Virgil took a long, noisy slurp, draining his beer. "I don't know where to start."

"Where'd you serve?" Rich offered.

"England."

"What branch?"

Tom came up with two beers, setting one before Virgil, the second by Stephen. "That's $7 for the two."

"That's okay, Tom," Rich said with his hand up.

"Thanks, Keeper." Virgil held up the full glass and sipped.

"Grandpa flew in B-17s," Stephen added.

Tom picked up the empty glasses and took them to the sink.

"Eighth Air Force?"

"You bet, the Mighty Eighth. Best goddamn air force in the world."

"What years?"

"The tough years, '43 and '44."

"You fly?"

"Naw. I signed up at 16 straight off the farm and they put me in the tail."

"Tail? Tail gunner? Wow, Virgil, I am glad you're here to tell the story." This impressed Rich.

"I survived, good Lord willing."

"I have always wondered if the early B-17s had .30 caliber machine guns in the tail?"

"I started out with a single .30. Later B-17s had one .50 caliber. Then I got twin .50s in late '44. Those did some damage to the Luftwaffe boys." Virgil laughed, almost to himself. "We were wild, just a bunch of crazy fucking kids.

Me, I was walking beans one year, the next I'm in London, England, drinking, jitterbugging, dodging buzz bombs at night, then plastering Berlin in the daytime."

"Best time of your life?"

Virgil shyly smiled, his eyes twinkling. "You're fuckin' well told," he softly said, taking a drink. "I even seen the first jet fighter."

"ME 262s? That must've been quite a sight."

"Scared the hell out of us. We couldn't figure out how the damn thing flew with no propeller."

"Fast?"

"I don't know if I ever put a shot in any of 'em." He chuckled. "They would lay back, just out of range, hiding in the contrails. When the escort peeled off they would swoop in, wave after wave of the bastards."

"Was '43 the first Schweinfurt raid?"

"I was on both. That was rough. We lost a lot of good men."

"Virgil, you have my respect and eternal gratitude for all you did." Rich held out his hand. He gently took the old man's narrow bony hand in his and shook it.

"Like I said, we were kids. We just knew we didn't want Hitler running the show."

"Grandpa's pretty modest."

"I've talked to a lot of World War Two guys; nearly all are modest about what they did. And all they did was save the world." Rich smiled. "Virgil, you're welcome here any time."

"Thanks, Keeper." Virgil held up a couple of dollars. "Here, put this in the tip jar. You guys are A-OK."

Richie Valens faded to Los Lobos' *Come On, Let's Go.*

"Sounds to me like Jorge got to pick some tunes," Rich whispered to Tom as he passed behind him.

Tom grinned and nodded.

Activity, conversation and all but the music playing seemed to pause throughout the bar. Rich glanced up from washing glasses in the bar sink. A slender man wearing a tailored gray suit stood framed in the doorway. He wore mirrored lens aviator sunglasses, reflecting the blinking colored lights and LCDs from the bar room. Rich scanned the room and noted a variety of expressions on people, from curiosity to disdain. The man's head swept side to side, for all appearances checking the crowd. Obviously, this was the law and a few people shrank from his gaze. Rich shook the water from a glass and set it upside down on the folded towel. He wiped his hands, watching and waiting. He knew where the shot gun leaned under the bar, just in case.

"I'm looking for Keeper," the gray suit said to Tom.

Tom made an arching motion with his hand, pointing down the bar to Rich.

With both hands, the man carefully removed his sunglasses and started toward Rich. "I'm looking for Keeper?"

His head cocked sideways, the corners of his mouth drawn down, Rich regarded the man a moment, saying nothing. In the semi-dark his face looked young, a mite too young.

"That's me. And you are...?"

"FBI Agent Paul Bertoloni."

"Ah," Rich straightened up.

Bertoloni looked around the bar. "Is there someplace more private we can talk?"

Rich motioned to the side room, with the pool table. "We can go in there. You want something to drink?"

"A Coke would be fine."

"I'll let Tom know." Rich stepped over to Tom.

"Who the hell's that?" Tom whispered. "Looks like a lawyer or..."

"...or a Fed?"

"Yeah."

Some Hispanic men from a table got up quickly and left.

"Have Daisy bring over a Coke."

"Just the one?"

"Ask her to see if Jorge's got a pot of coffee on. I'll have a cup."

Bertoloni sat at a small round table in the corner. Two young Asians moved about the dark edges surrounding the center lit pool table, their boisterous back and forth banter turned subdued under the agent's steady stare.

Rich got a chair across from the agent and leaned his back to the wall. "Thanks for coming in. It's nice to meet you agent."

Billiard balls clacked and thumped against the bumpers of the pool table.

"Likewise." Bertoloni reached into his inside pocket. "Call me Paul."

Rich noted an arrogance about the younger man's gestures. With a slight flourish he produced a shiny brown leather wallet from his inside jacket pocket and plucked a white business card from a clip. The other side held a blue photo ID card.

"I'm Rich, Richard Rice," he quietly said, behind his palm, not wanting anyone to hear. He knew it was inappropriate to use his standard introduction of 'I'm Rich...Richie...Richard...don't-call-me-Dick, Rice.' "Can I see your ID?" Rich took the offered business card.

Bertoloni opened the wallet and showed Rich his ID.

They shook hands, gripping a little too tightly.

"Okay, Rich."

"I would appreciate it if you continued to call me Keeper. Especially around here."

Bertoloni half-smiled and winked, "Gotcha." He tucked the wallet back in his pocket and smoothed down his red and white diagonal striped tie.

"Here we are." Daisy came up with a small tray, setting a round cardboard coaster and tall glass of Coke before Bertoloni. She put a heavy white porcelain mug of coffee by Rich's hand. "Just the way you like it, Boss."

"Thank you," the agent said.

"Thanks, Daisy."

She tucked the tray on her hip, asking "Anything else I can get you?"

"We're good."

Bertoloni nodded, tilting the glass of Coke to his mouth.

"Give a shout if you need me." Daisy spun and noticing the pool players, stopped. "Another round?"

Taking a beer bottle off the rails, one turned up the bottle and drank. "Sure." The other replied.

"Be right back."

"Tidy little operation you got here. Good people. But..." The agent gave a grimace. "The Ordinary?"

Rich grinned, twisting the mug around for its handle. "I get a mix of people, locals and a Metro Community College crowd." He sipped coffee. "I didn't want a name with any attitude. The Ordinary is a phrase used in colonial times. I am the Keeper of an Ordinary."

"Clever." Bertoloni leaned over the table and with his index finger he moved aside the lapel of Rich's flannel over shirt. The butt of the .45 automatic in its shoulder holster became visible. Keeping his eyes on the agent, Rich let him take a peek, then moved away.

"You got a permit for that antique?"

"For this?" Rich checked aside at the pool players. They were engrossed in racking a new game and chalking their cue sticks. "Family heirloom. It was my dad's."

"One of the best ever—up to 50 yards. Sort of heavy and bulky though." The agent's expression tightened, becoming serious. "What other kinds of protection you got?"

"I got a conceal carry for a Smith & Wesson .38. Small enough I can wear it in a holster inside my waist band."

"You got a stopper in your arm pit, but that .38 isn't going to help you much."

"I've got a couple of 12 gauge shotguns, one sawed off."

"You know you're not supposed to do that."

"I'm not supposed to get shot at either."

"I didn't hear any of that."

"And I have my dad's 1903 Springfield."

"Another museum piece. Scoped?"

"Yeah. 4 X."

"Nice." Bertoloni paused, took a deep breath and thoughtfully pursed his lips. "But I have to tell you, that's not nearly enough fire power to fight off the people after you."

"Oh yeah?" Rich lowered his coffee cup.

"These guys are ex-Soviet military or KGB, or just mafia type thugs and they have modified Zastavas, Glocks, M4s, Kalashnikovs, you name it."

"I'm thinking they're not going to find me."

"The place isn't in your name?"

"Nope. It's all incorporated under my wife's maiden name, Gisele Esslin." Rich held up his hand and counted on his fingers his precautions. "I don't use my real name anywhere. I pay with cash. I have throwaway mobile phones. All emails and files are encrypted through Telegram on the Tor browser. This place, the bank account, car and insurance, all in my wife's name. And I am known only as Keeper." Rich dropped his head a moment. "My vehicle is registered in Nebraska, under my wife's name. I only have two things in my name—a driver's license, which is still valid, and gun permit."

"Is she with you? Your wife? They could track you through her."

"She's not. She lives in Illinois. And, they think I was shot and killed."

"You on the deep net, the Onion router?"

Rich nodded with silence and a stare. His suspicions rose. He didn't like talking about this.

"I'll take that as a yes. No internet foot print? No Facebook? No Twitter or Pinterest? No social media at all? No bank info? You're fairly incognito. I'd say you're in decent shape. Have you heard from Dedmon?"

"That guy?" Rich replied with a confused expression on his face. "No, not me, not since he dropped me off at my wife's mother's in Glencoe. Why?"

"Glencoe?"

"That's where my wife is." Damn, Rich thought, I am saying too much.

"Okay."

"What's the deal with him? He called my wife recently. She said she didn't know where I was."

"That was smart. Let me know if he keeps bugging your wife and somehow locates you."

"You'll be the first."

"Call in your phone number every time you get a new mobile."

"Okay."

"I'm going to set up a meeting with Omaha Police for you and me. A detective or Omaha PD will come by and let you know when. First, I want you to call my office. I have the name of an armorer that can set you up with a Glock. That's so I don't have to worry about you waving a newspaper sword at these bad guys with their AKs."

"They might laugh themselves to death."

"My bosses know about you and your situation and they have signed off on me looking out for you."

"Thanks."

"We're going to want something in return." Bertoloni gave Rich a tight-lipped smile.

"What?" Rich tensed.

The agent set himself on his elbows, his eyes boring across at Rich, and spoke quietly and precisely. "You have names and addresses of contacts inside Bratva, working within the U.S. They gave you information that helped you with the newspaper articles on prostitution and human trafficking. We'll want those names. And any dark web IP addresses you have as well. Not now, but definitely later."

Rich simmered a moment in silence. "I won't reveal my sources."

"You be like that. I want to get these guys," Bertoloni grinned, wide. "We'll talk later...deal?"

"Have you found who killed Bill More?"

"Who's Bill More?"

"My editor at the Park Forest Daily." Bertoloni's carelessness angered Rich. "You told me he was killed."

"Okay. The editor guy...I recall," Bertoloni raked his fingers through his hair and pinched his nose thoughtfully. "He was killed in a burglary at the paper. No, nothing yet."

"And the guy that took a shot at me?"

The agent shrugged his shoulders. "Got some leads. I'll get him." He smiled smug.

"Nothing?" Rich's jaw grew taut, irritated by the agent's response.

"When we meet up with Omaha police, I'll have more." The ice cubes crashed to the bottom of the glass as Bertoloni finished his Coke. He stood, shaking and smoothing the lapels of his suit jacket. He shot the cuffs.

"Thanks." They shook hands again.

"All right, Keeper. Take care."

Rich reached back and plucked the empty glass, napkin and coffee mug off the table. He fought the urge to throw the glass and cup against the wall.

Jorge came out of the kitchen, standing in the doorway. Bertoloni saw him and his eyes narrowed. When Jorge noticed the agent eyeing him, he looked away and backed into the kitchen.

"What's that all about?" Rich asked Jorge as he came into the kitchen and put the glass and mug in the sink.

"What all about, *Jefe*?"

"You know that guy?"

"The suit? Naw."

"I don't know if that guy's a piece of shit," Rich mumbled to himself watching Bertoloni leave. "Or a gold-plated piece of shit." He turned back to Jorge. "Okay. How we doing tonight?"

"*Es bueno, Jefe.* Nachos, *grande* nachos, nachos *vamos.*"

Carlos Santana's opening notes of *Black Magic Woman* pierced through the conversations in the bar room.

"Seems to be Jorge's music day."

Jorge chuckled. "*Si. Senor* Tom bamboozled."

"Tell Tom I will be out for a couple of hours." Rich said. "I need some air. I might take Roommate for a walk, then do some paperwork. If you guys need me I'm at the number I gave you."

"*Si, Jefe.*"

"I'll be back for dinner later."

"*Nos vemos.*"

Rich walked a long time into the neon bright night, up one side of 24th and down the other with Roommate barely keeping up at the end of his leash. They weaved through pedestrians not stopping for anything or anyone. The small dog was famished when they got back. He gobbled up the dry food in his bowl and collapsed on the couch. Rich powered up his laptop on the table in the living room, waiting not so patiently as the operating system booted. Then he logged onto his encryption program and clicked the email icon.

"Gisele," he typed. "So glad we got to talk. Just could not stop thinking about you. Hate being apart, worse than ever.

FBI agent came in and we talked. I've met some FBI guys before. This one's young and ambitious. He wants something from me. We went over my precautions and he seems to think I was doing okay remaining anonymous and out of sight. I am going to the FBI office and meet with him and the Omaha Police about protecting me."

His mood improved, pouring it out in an email to Gisele.

"He asked about that guy Dedmon, just like on the phone before. There's something weird about that guy. Be careful."

"And...good news, babe. Clear your appointments for Monday until Thursday in two weeks. I'll text you directions and an address where we can meet. Yeah, it's going to happen. Pack for a couple of days. Don't tell anyone, even your mother. I can't wait to see you. I am going to bring my Roommate also."

"Love you."

Rich read over the email, deleting "He wants something from me." That would worry Gisele. He clicked SEND.

Chapter 8

Something brushed across Rich's knee.

Rich lifted his head from his arm, blinking at sun splashed windows. He'd fallen asleep at the table. Roommate had a paw on his leg. The small dog's big brown eyes gazed up at Rich, his pink tongue out as he huffed through his parted mouth. Still in yesterday's clothes, Rich snapped off the light and stretched.

Weeks had passed since the meeting at the FBI office. The tension remained ratcheted tight.

"Roomy." Rich wiped sleep from his eyes. "I guess I drifted off." He pet Roommate's head.

The computer woke from sleep mode on a Reuters page Rich researched about human trafficking in Armenia. Rich sifted through pages and stopped on his reservation. He logged onto Tor, encrypting an email to Gisele.

Today: 6 PM – Mrs. Esslin

94 to 90

39/51 @ Rockford

20W

Mississippi – Dubuque

3/52N – X Peru Rd
Peru Rd to Indian Mounds Lane – cabin

He moved the cursor to the SEND icon and tapped the pad. He knew Gisele would decipher the message and understand.

Roommate scratched at the back door. Rich checked the surveillance camera. It looked clear. He picked up the bank bag from the pantry floor then let Roommate in.

"Got a lot to do, Rooms...get things ready." He placed a bowl of food down. The dog scampered over. "Going to meet our pretty lady tonight."

Rich packed carelessly and quickly, throwing clothing and his shaving kit into a small nylon back pack. More thoughtfully, he put the bank bag in the gun safe and selected which weapons to bring. He set the Glock 32 aside, the .38 Smith & Wesson to wear on his hip and the Bushmaster. Gisele needed to shoot the new weapons. He slipped the weapons in a desert beige canvas bag, with boxes of ammo in the pockets. At the bottom of the gun safe lay a manila envelope fat with a reporter's notebook, yellow tablets of scribbles and assorted thumb drives. A lot of people wanted what was in that envelope. Rich pondered a moment, then put the envelope in the gun case.

Roommate sat in the kitchen, licking his chops and watching Rich hustle about the apartment.

He caught sight of the dog watching. "Hey Roomy," he said. "Ready for a ride?"

The dog followed Rich as he went to the dumb waiter and climbed down. "Be back up in a minute," he called looking down the dark shaft. Roommate whimpered.

Single lights glowed in the kitchen. Silence hung over the bar room. Rich checked behind the bar and into the kitchen. Standing with hands on hips, he couldn't help feeling apprehensive about leaving—even for a few days. The Ordinary had been his sanctuary, his safe house, his Alamo.

He scribbled a note for Tom, explaining he would be gone for a couple of days, adding a contact number. Rich took a handful of beers and a couple of bottles of champagne--French vintage, from the bar. In the kitchen refrigerator Jorge had prepared dinners and other food. The foil wrapped plates may not have been for Rich, but he packed them in a cooler anyway.

Loading up his truck, he left Roommate for last. The small black and white dog jumped down the iron steps to the parking lot. Rich locked the apartment and followed. He put the pet carrier in the back and lifting Roommate up. The animal dog paddled through the air landing on the passenger seat.

"You know Rooms," Rich said as he got in and turned the ignition. "That's Gisele's seat." The electric gate slowly drew back. Rich drove out and looked back making sure the gate reclosed. He sped up to the limit, driving onto the I-80 on ramp and merging into the flow of traffic.

He realized, driving east over the Missouri River, the last time he was on this stretch of interstate he was heading west to save his life. Rich clenched his teeth and wondered if it would ever end. Now he drove back, closer to the danger.

Roommate lay curled on the seat, lulled to slumber by the rhythm of the road. Rich reached over and gave him a couple of affectionate pats. The little dog gave him comfort.

A well-traveled road, with constant traffic, driving toward Des Moines made Rich feel exposed. He fought the notion that every vehicle with Illinois tags might be Russian Mafia, or Suka's gang, looking for him. Impossible he told himself as he wrestled the futility of repressing the thought.

At Des Moines he looped around onto Highway 35 North. No longer on the main road gave him a measure of relief. He didn't scan every other car for someone out to kill him. Beyond Des Moines, the highway turned into long stretches of undeveloped land, interspersed with industrial parks and farms.

Highway 35 North passed through small towns and sights but Highway 30 East, by comparison, seemed desolation row broken up by clusters of tall white windmills. From the GPS display Rich noted only Marshalltown halfway to Cedar Rapids as the largest congregation of businesses and people. Between these semi-urban centers little else existed other than gently rolling farm lands. Late summer corn stood high, rich green stalks with fat ears and long yellow tassels. An elephant could gaze down the neat rows, eyes to ears.

The road changed from a four-lane divided highway to two-lane cement slabs. Rich saw few other vehicles down the long ribbon of road dissected by faded yellow dashes. Occasionally though he would come upon slow moving farm equipment, harvesters, combines and tractors, were assembling for sowing the ripening fields.

Roommate sat up and fidgeted. A dog owner's intuition told Rich to pull off the highway at an abandoned weigh station. He parked, put Roommate on a leash, and carried him down to the pavement. The dog sniffed around the overgrown weeds sprouting from cracks in the large square sections of concrete. He lifted his leg on the corner of the red brick booth. Rich shaded his eyes and peered in the window. Graffiti dressed the walls and an overturned chair, newspapers and fast food litter filled the narrow empty building.

Rich squinted, looking back as the late afternoon sun fell to the west.

"Empty?" He asked Roommate. The dog all but ignored him, sniffing around the brick base. The scent must've been good as Roommate circled, then squatted. Shaking slightly, the dog squeezed out a rumpled blackish turd that plopped to the paving.

"That's a pungent one, Rooms. C'mon, let's head back to the truck."

Rich filled a bowl of cool water and set it down for the dog to drink.

The low orange sun flashed in the rear view mirrors of the truck. Rich set out a bowl of dry food and a second bowl of cool water. In the cooler, the two green glass necks and gold foil tops of the champagne sticking out of the white mound of ice made Rich smile.

They made good time. Rich would arrive at the inn well ahead of Gisele.

Cedar Rapids came up almost like a sudden interruption of the vast Iowa acreage of corn and soybeans. Not much to shout about as a metro area. Highway 30 went through the "city" in a couple of blinks. Rich started to relax, in motion and hurtling along under the anonymity of the road. On the other side of Cedar Rapids farms resumed, with fields, barns and silos bluntly rising from the crops. The verdant uniformity of gentle waves of tall corn gave way to industrial parks, enclaves of new home construction and strip malls as Rich neared Dubuque. Traffic increased in pace and volume.

"Coming into Dubuque, Roomy."

The dog got up and stretched, looking around. A car sped by, startling Roommate. He cast worrisome eyes over to Rich driving.

"Easy, pup. It's all right." Rich scratched his head. "Lay back down. You're okay."

The highway climbed up, though not steeply, rather in a long gradual ascent. Long haul semis labored, angling into turnout lanes at the first opportunity. Rich pushed the gas pedal, gathering speed past slower cars.

The road came out on a high bluff overlooking the wide Mississippi River and the city of Dubuque spread west from the edge of the river up to and over the bluffs. A fair-sized city, Dubuque had a visible downtown area with office blocks and modest high rises of six to eight stories. Here and there red brick church steeples dotted the mixed business and residential neighborhoods. A shadow crept east over the city from the base of the bluffs. With the setting sun the waters of the Mississippi turned an olive green, with glittering peaks. Tiny boats cut white vees close to the banks. A modern wide eight-lane trestle humpback highway bridge carrying traffic into and out of Dubuque to the south. A green two-lane bridge, looking like a child's erector set, arched across the big river to the north. Cars and trucks busily beetled eastward and into the west over the bridges.

"We're here, Rooms."

Descending down the bluffs Rich scanned passing signs. "There...US 151 North." A quick head check and he moved to the right lane. He eased onto 151 on a wide overpass.

"Another 10 miles."

Rich's thoughts went to Gisele, who, if all went according to plan, should be an hour away, driving west.

He couldn't suppress the smile. A glance to the console and Rich picked his mobile phone from the cup holder. Another dip of his eyes and he scrolled down the contacts to G, and pressed send. It rang twice, then connected.

"Hello?" Background noise distorted her voice.

"Gisele," Rich spoke loud. "Where are you?"

"East of Rockford," Her voice crackled with excitement. "I can't wait to see you."

"Me too. Did you understand the directions?"

"Got'em. I should be there in an hour's time. Love you."

"Love you too. Call if you have a problem."

They clicked off at the same time.

US 151 North rolled along the top of the bluffs, heading into preserves and park areas. He turned onto Highway 3, a narrow road and slowed at the Peru Road crossroads. The road snaked into a lush green forest.

"This is cool," Rich said to Roommate.

A wooden sign loomed ahead reading Indian Mounds Inn with an arrow. Rich turned off and went down the narrow tree-lined country lane. After nearly a mile, the blacktop broke out of the preserve. A long gray stone two-story Cape Cod style structure stood in the midst of a grassy clearing. An ornate frontier-style sign at the head of a circular drive announced Indian Mounds Inn. The clearing couldn't have been more that 20 yards deep on three sides of the inn. Trees lined the edge of the bluffs. Beyond was the Mississippi River and views of Wisconsin. A line of small natural wood constructed cabins accessible by rutted dirt road faced the bluffs. Rich parked at the entrance to the inn.

Roommate sat up and shook, smacking.

"You stay here, Rooms." Rich lowered the driver and passenger side windows an inch or so. He got out and stretched, shaking his limbs to loosen them from the hours of driving. A number of cars with an assortment of state plates were parked in a side lot. Rich looked over the tags. No Illinois plates.

He climbed the flagstone steps and pushed open the heavy carved oak and stained glass door. The oriental carpeted living room was decorated in an old world style with blue velvet wing chairs and a flower print overstuffed couch. A soot-stained gray brick fireplace, with wood mantle dominated the sidewall. The walls were papered in pink brocade, framed in rich dark molding. Chamber music played softly while a German designed grandfather's clock ticked loudly with each swing of its brass pendulum. A dining area on the other side of a flight of stairs was populated by older men and women quietly chatting and eating. Tucked in a corner at the base of the stairs was the front desk and check in. A youngish man worked there, distracted by a game on the computer screen.

"Excuse me." Rich said. "You have a cabin reserved for Mr. and Mrs. Esslin?"

He had long brown hair in a ponytail and wore wire rim spectacles. Reluctantly, he left the game and stood. "Mmmmm let me check." He minimized the screen on the computer and brought up a page.

A middle-aged pair, two men, came side by side down the carpeted steps. One gave Rich a sly eye. As they passed a scent vaguely like kitchen cleanser followed.

"Ahhhh yes. Three night stay in cabin four." He pulled a sheet out from under the counter and with a pen set it before Rich. "Mmmm may I see your license and a major credit card."

Rich took the sheet and filled in R and G Esslin, skipping the address line and car make and license number. He scrawled round and long lines on the signature field. Putting the pen down, he patted his back pocket. "Ah, shoot. I seem to have left my driver's license and credit card in my vehicle. I plan to pay cash anyway."

"Mmmm cash?"

"Yeah." Rich gave him a look as if paying cash was nothing unusual. "A hundred and forty-three dollars a night...right?" He dug out a thick fold of green bills from his front pocket. "Four hundred and twenty nine dollars total. That includes pet fee."

"There's a hotel tax." He turned back to the computer. "Mmmm your total is four hundred and fifty three dollars."

Rich slowly peeled off one, two, three, four, five hundred dollar bills, tantalizing the young man's eyes fixed on the wad of bills in his hand. He fanned out the hundreds on the counter, pocketing the fold and waited.

"Mmmm thanks." The clerk carefully scooped the bills and put them under a tray in a drawer. He pinched out two twenties, a five and two ones from slots in the trays. He slowly counted out the money on the counter, then took keys from a wall of hooks behind him.

Rich had his change in hand as the man put the keys on the counter.

"Cabin four. Ahhhh you didn't fill out the registration completely." The man placed a receipt on the counter.

"I'll fill it out later." Rich snatched the keys with his right hand and flipped them to his left, taking the receipt.

"Mmmm, I think I need this filled out..."

"Let me settle in," Rich said, backing toward the door. "I'll be back and fill it out...okay?" He opened the front door.

"Mmmm...but..."

Rich closed the door behind and briskly stepped down the stairs and around the front of his truck. Roommate sat in the driver's seat. "Are you driving, or me?" He opened the door. "C'mon, quick getaway." The small dog jumped over the console to the passenger seat. Rich hopped in. The truck roared as Rich drove through the lot to the dirt road leading to the cabins. The last cabin had a wood number 4 under a yellow bug light. He pulled past, then backed up, parking between cabins 2 and 3.

Shutting off the engine, Rich picked up his phone. He scrolled down to "G" and texted: "Cabin 4...end." He pressed SEND.

Taking down the pet carrier from the bed of the pickup, Rich carefully set Roommate inside and locked the cage door. The dog looked forlornly out the crisscross bars, whining.

'Oh hush, it's only until we get inside."

The light from the open door cut the darkness inside the cabin. He found the switch on the wall and clicked on an overhead light. He put the pet cage down and went back out to the truck. He unloaded the cooler, his bags and the box of provisions. Roommate had his nose pressed against the bars, checking the air of the cabin.

Rich surveyed the pine wood paneled rustic cabin. One large room with fireplace, flat screen TV, couch and sitting section opened to a counter and narrow kitchen. The rest of the cabin consisted of a bedroom with shiny brass bed and large bay window that featured an easterly view of the bluffs and big river beyond. While quaint, the tiled bath had a Jacuzzi, double sinks, toilet and uncommonly, a bidet. Rich walked through the cabin lifting blinds and pulling back curtains. Soft late afternoon light filled the rooms. He closed and latched the hook on the screen door, then let Roommate out of the carrier.

"Check it out, Roomy." The small dog hopped out and started sniffing.

Rich's phone buzzed on the counter. A text balloon from Gisele popped on screen. "F@*king traffic. Be there soon. Love." Silently, Rich laughed. "That's my girl," he muttered.

Jorge had put together plates of enchiladas, rice and beans, foil wrapped and ready to be heated. He had added salads in sealed containers, salsa and slices of cheesecake. Rich stowed the bottles of champagne in the refrigerator, along with an assortment of soft drinks and a six of Negro Modelo and Especial.

"Rooms?" The dog bounded out of the bedroom. "You stay there." Rich wagged his finger as he backed out the screen door.

Roommate ran after Rich, stopping at the screen and watching Rich pull out the long canvas case from the back seat of the truck. The dog followed Rich into the bedroom, watching as he pushed the canvas case under the bed.

A small flagstone tile patio, with round table and chairs at the back of the cabin faced the bluffs and river. Rich led Roommate on the leash. The dog inspected every tree and shrub, lifting his leg at the base of a bush, peeing for a long time.

The magnificent view distracted Rich.

"Hey handsome—know where a gal can get a drink around here?"

Rich wheeled around. "Sweetness!"

Gisele came out the back door of the cabin.

They fell into each other's arms, lips fitting tight and perfect.

"Oh, shit, I missed your arms," she whispered.

"You feel so good."

Roommate finished peeing and looked up at Rich and Gisele, his round head tilted to one side, then the other.

Rich kissed her neck and slid his mouth to her waiting lips. "Ahhhhhhh...."

Their warm and wet tongues teased.

Rich began to get aroused. Gisele noticed.

"You did miss me."

"God, yes," Rich beamed, squeezing her.

Gisele's lean, lithe body radiated desire in a loose fitting embroidered white peasant blouse and pleated green shorts. Athletic but not muscle bound, Gisele's shoulders crossed her tall frame in a perfect "T". Her torso went straight to her narrow hips from which tanned slender legs were supported by two noticeably large feet. Her feet were best left unmentioned. She had pushed her tortoiseshell framed sunglasses up, holding back her mid-length honey colored wavy blonde hair. A broad smile gave her Nordic oval face a glow. Sparkles emanated from Gisele's blue green eyes; eyes that danced with happiness.

"You left the back door open. Not a good idea."

"I expected you"

"Are those your ribs I feel?"

"Maybe."

Gisele swayed back. Her eyes narrowed. "You're looking...gaunt."

Rich exhaled. "The tension...and stress.

"Don't I know it." They embraced. "Why do I have the feeling we're being watched?"

"What?" Rich started. He quickly checked the surroundings.

"Is this your roommate?" Gisele nodded her head down.

"Oh...yeah. Where's my manners. Roomy, let me introduce you to the most beautiful girl in the world."

Gisele went down on one knee and pet Roommate. The black and white dog panted and licked Gisele's hand. "You're quite the cutie."

Rich stood above. Gisele wasn't wearing a bra. His eyes were drawn down her blouse, mesmerized by her small firm breasts and pointy brown nipples.

"...and he's not hearing a word I say," Gisele cooed to Roommate. "Dad's staring down at my boobs. I like that...very much." Gisele rose, close to Rich. "Still my bad boy?"

"I try, Gis," he replied. "C'mon, let's bring your stuff in and have something to eat."

"This is really a nice place." She trailed Rich and Roommate into the cabin.

"It's sort of remote. I think we'll be safe."

"Ummm," she paused at the counter. "I didn't just feel your ribs...are you carrying a gun?"

Rich stopped at the screen door, looking back. "Always."

"You fucking need it?"

"Yes."

"Okay, babe...I guess." Gisele opened the refrigerator, bent down and pulled out a beer.

Coming back in with Gisele's bags, Rich said: "Jorge made some enchiladas for dinner."

Gisele took the beer bottle from her lips. "So I'm finally going to eat something cooked by the hombre whose paychecks I've been signing all this time?"

"Uh huh." Rich dropped Gisele's bags on the bed. "You'll find out he's a damned good cook."

"Speaking of cooking...C'mere babe." Smiling, Gisele ground her hips against his as they kissed. "Damn, I missed you."

He warmed the enchilada dinners in the microwave while Gisele set the table on the patio. The setting sun made the air cool. A slight humid breeze rustled the tops of the pine trees. Roommate, his leash tied to a chair leg, munched from his bowl. They sat and ate.

"I brought," Gisele started, wiping her mouth, "papers and assorted legal documents related to The Ordinary."

"You know I can't sign anything." Rich shoveled a forkful of rice into his mouth.

"Know that. I have spreadsheets breaking down the money coming in and what's going back into our IRA."

"I trust you."

"Do me a favor?"

"What?"

"Take off the gun."

"Nope. Can't."

Gisele drank beer, staring over the bottle at Rich. His tight expression wasn't defiance, more matter of fact. Sighing, she let it go, falling back in her chair. "That was good. Your man, Jorge, is a good cook."

"He has some other goodies for us."

"Like what?"

"Cheesecake and I've also some French champagne for later." Rich put his plate down for Roommate to lick.

Gisele watched Roomy clean the plate. "You spoil that little shit."

"That little shit is the only thing that keeps me sane without you."

Dusk softly descended on the Mississippi River Valley. Clouds in the blue sky turned golden as lights glowed along the riverbank and throughout Dubuque on the flats below the bluffs. A paddle wheeler, with twin gold tipped smoke stacks, chugged up river.

"What are our plans for tomorrow?"

"Either hike the trails on the bluffs or go downtown."

"Trails tomorrow," Gisele polished off her beer. "Downtown, the day after."

"That's a plan. I'd like to take you out to the country and do some shooting."

"Pass."

Roommate finished Rich's plate and smacking his lips sat at Gisele's feet.

"Honey, you need to..."

"What do you call him? Roomy? Rooms?"

"Yeah." Rich let Gisele avoid the subject.

"What do you want, Roomy?"

The little dog scratched behind his ear with his hind foot.

Gisele put her plate down and Roommate stepped to it.

A knock sounded on the front door. Rich turned, crouched, his hand sliding to his hip, squinting. "Shit." He recognized the clerk at the screen door, registration in hand.

"Who's that?" Gisele whispered.

"The clerk. He's got the registration."

"You didn't register?"

"I bull rushed him. I can't."

"Gotcha." Gisele wadded up the napkin, tossed it on her plate and got up. "I tell you what. I'll get rid of him—you fill the Jacuzzi and open a bottle of champagne."

"Deal."

Gisele snapped on the overhead light and crossed the cabin to the door. "Who the hell are you?"

"Oh, ah, the mmmm, desk clerk."

"And...what do you want?"

"Um, mmm Mister Esslin didn't fill out the registration."

"Oh, he's so absentminded some times. Give it here, I'm Mrs. Esslin." Gisele partly opened the screen door and snatched the sheet from the clerk's hand. "I'll fill it out." She slammed the screen door and turned away.

"Bbbbut," he stammered and stood. "Bbbbring it to me." Defeated, he slouched away.

Roommate trotted in. Water sounded filling the Jacuzzi in the bathroom. Rich, behind the counter, twisted loose the wire cage on the champagne bottle. "Good job, Gis." With his thumbs he worked loose the cork until it shot off with a loud pop.

She slapped the registration on the counter. "Let's get out of these clothes..."

"...and into a warm Jacuzzi." Rich poured.

They lay, Gisele's back to Rich's front, in the steaming hot water. Candlelight cast the room in a soft golden hue. Rich's arms encircled Gisele's naked body. Her head lay back on his shoulder. He kissed her warm, wet neck.

"Want the jets on?"

"No. This is heaven."

For five months, since the sniper attack had wounded him, Rich had been rigid with wariness and fear. He felt as if he were held in the tight grip of a fist. Every breath came difficult and constricted, each action calculated, a night's sleep rare. He let out a slow, measured sigh expelling just about all the tension binding him.

"Look at that little guy," Gisele said with a giggle, peering over the edge of the Jacuzzi at Roommate curled on the bathroom throw.

"He's a good dog." Rich sipped champagne.

""He is. But shit...he's got quite the under bite." Gisele swung about in the bath. "Should've named him Bruce." On all fours she kissed Rich.

Rich shivered. Her long glistening wet body excited him. He pinched her nipples, gently rolling each in his fingers. She wiggled slightly and moaned softly, deep in her throat. Her hand found him.

"Dammit, honey. I can't wait." Gisele slid her knees up, on either side of his hips. Slowly, she squatted down, guiding him into her. "I almost forgot how blue your eyes were."

"Oh, baby." Rich rolled his head back. "I missed you."

For the longest time they held their hips tightly joined. Rich brought her face to his lips and tenderly they kissed. The long drought made them hungry, quickly. Almost involuntarily their bodies started to move together, then in collision that grew with intensity.

Water splashed on the bathroom tile. Roommate flinched and sat up.

There was no holding back. Gentle kisses became urgent and greedy. Gisele gripped Rich's shoulders hard. He had his hands clutching her hips, pulling her to him.

Gisele surrendered first, convulsing with a pleasured groan. Rich met her at the peak of her climax. They shook and shuddered as one. For a long time they held each other, getting their breath back, becoming tender once more. "God, I love you."

"Let me see it," Gisele said.

Rich gave her a questioning look. "See it?"

"The scar."

"Oh." Rich brought his arm around. Water dripped over a raised berm of whitish skin down his shoulder and side. Gisele's fingers traced the length of the scar.

"Is this bullshit ever going to end?"

"It will, Gis. They'll get caught or forget about me."

She gave him a quick kiss and sat back, drinking champagne. "Glad you think so."

Roommate put a tentative paw on the edge of the Jacuzzi and whimpered.

"You little perv." Gisele patted the dog's head. "You watched us the whole time."

Rich chuckled. "We made quite a mess, babe."

"I know. Wasn't it great?"

Roommate briskly walked out of the bathroom, then came back looking at Rich.

"I think he needs to go out."

Gisele stepped out and wound a towel around her chest. It was just long enough. "I'll take him." She tucked a corner of the towel in the front. "Any more champagne?" Gisele followed Roommate.

Rich slowly climbed out, almost slipping on the wet floor. "I think so." Toweling off, he leaned out the bathroom door. He noticed Gisele take her purse from the table and let the dog out the back door. "Why would she take her purse?" he thought. Rich laid towels on the floor to soak up the water, wrapped a towel round his waist and poured what was left of the champagne into two flutes. With a glass in each hand, he opened the door with his shoulder. "Here we..."

Startled, Gisele turned away and blew smoke out of her mouth.

"...go." Rich stood. "When did you start smoking?" He set the flutes down. In a way he felt embarrassed for her.

"Shit." She crossed her arms and flicked an ash. "A couple of days after you left." Roommate scratched around the base of a tree. "I just couldn't deal with it."

Rich went up to her and put his arms around her waist. He forced her evasive eyes to settle on his. "It's okay, Gis."

"I know you hate it."

"Both my parent died from smoking. Let's not talk about it. I do understand why."

"What did the FBI say?" Gisele brought up.

He pulled out a chair and sat. "They lost track of Nikolai Franko."

"The bastard that shot you?"

"The one."

"This is bullshit. Are we going to have to live like this for the rest of our lives?" Gisele took a long drag, tilting her head back spewing a jet of blue smoke toward the starry crown of the night sky.

Roommate sniffed Rich's foot.

"They want to get him for attempted murder. If they pick him up for pandering and trafficking he'll be back on the street in six months."

"Why don't they leave us alone?"

"I've got something they want?"

"What?" Gisele angrily stubbed her cigarette on the corner of a chair. Red sparks spilled to the patio.

"My notes and sources for my articles on Russian sex trafficking in the Midwest. I also have IP addresses for the hidden web sites they use."

"Why don't you just give it to them?"

"No way. That wouldn't end it with the Russians. The FBI guy is young and ambitious. He wants the big bust so he can move up. I'm not sure he wouldn't dangle me out there to get the Russians to bite. It's like I'm standing between the trenches in No Man's Land."

Conversation and laughter sounded a couple of cabins over. A group of people, carrying drinks and talking came out to the patio behind their cabin. Rich and Gisele looked at each other, then the towels they wore.

"Get the champagne." Rich hissed, scooping up Roommate.

Too late, they were spotted. "Oh, is this area clothing optional?" someone yelled, followed by laughter.

Scurrying in the back door, Gisele and Rich were unable to suppress embarrassed giggles. Rich caught her as she ran in. He kissed her mouth.

"Shit, I forgot my purse." Gisele took a deep breath, girded her towel and strutted out the door with all the exaggerated movements of a high society dame. She went to the table, picked up her purse and with a haughty look, made a tight pirouette and walked back. Whistles and cat calls, with a smattering of applause came from the far cabin. She blew them a kiss at the door.

That night they made love slowly. The urgency of their lust, built up over months apart gave way to languid expressions from their hearts. Lying naked with a gentle breeze billowing the lace curtains, moon light gave their bodies a shine. He moved down along her body, kissing. She gently moaned with each nibble and lick. When her back arched and hips rose up, she held her breath a long time, expelling a sigh. "Ohhhhhh."

They fell asleep, entwined.

In the quiet, Roommate jumped onto the bed and nosed around. He turned this way. He turned that way, finally settling between Rich and Gisele's legs. He exhaled deeply, contented. Little did Roommate know he was in for a bumpy night.

Chapter 9

Panicked, Rich sat up in bed. "Where's my gun?" He threw pillows off the head of the bed and rummaged through the nightstand drawers. "Roomy?"

"Rup," sounded from the kitchen.

Rich smelled bacon frying and coffee brewing. Jumping out of bed, he slipped on his jeans. Bending down, the soft canvas gun case lay stashed under the bed.

Gisele, arms folded across her chest, leaned against the sink. She wore Rich's white t-shirt and nothing else. Warily, she regarded him as he frantically stumbled out of the bedroom. Roommate sat on the counter, facing Gisele but with one long ear cocked back. His black and white head turned, watching Rich.

"Have you seen my gun?"

Eyes fixed on Rich, Gisele pointed to the counter next to her soft leatherette briefcase.

Audibly sighing, Rich snatched the Smith & Wesson .38 in its tanned leather holster.

"This bullshit has changed you." Gisele spoke in a hard tone.

She was right, but he didn't care. "Naw," he replied calmly.

"I'm cooking scrambled eggs and bacon and the coffee's about done." Gisele pushed off from the sink and poked at the sizzling bacon in the pan. Roommate watched her every move.

Rich sat on a stool on the other side of the counter.

Her back to him, Gisele forked up a dripping strip of rumpled brown bacon and laid it on a paper towel. "And I've fed Rooms and taken him out."

At the sound of his name, Roommate opened his mouth huffing, letting his pink tongue out and slightly lifting his right paw and then the left.

Halfway to the refrigerator Gisele stopped and said: "I might steal him from you. He's good people."

Rich rubbed his face in his hands, yet fully awake. "Not a chance. I told you Roomy's been the only other thing keeping me sane in this mess."

"Other?" Gisele took a carton of eggs and closed the refrigerator.

"Our emails...and calls."

"Good answer, Keeper." She cracked three eggs on the rim of a bowl, briskly whisking the contents with a fork. The eggs crackled and bubbled as she spilled yellow yolks into the pan. "By the way, I hate that name."

"Coffee ready?"

Gisele poured a cup and set it before Rich. "Aren't you forgetting something?"

Wide-eyed and blinking, Rich stared at her. It dawned on him. He went around the counter, took her hips in his hands and gave her a kiss.

"The eggs!" She broke the embrace and stirred the fluffy eggs.

Over breakfast, Gisele brought out a sheaf of legal papers from her briefcase.

"Holy crap, Gis," Rich exclaimed, chewing. "I'm not signing anything."

"I know, but you can take these back. These...." She pushed papers forward: "are forms for Jorge—proof of employment for his parole officer. This is a support order and wage garnishment for...." Gisele pursed her lips, raising her eyebrows and giving Rich a sidelong glance. "...Tom. I've got the truck registration. And," she elongated the short word. "We are getting small business tax credits this fiscal year; as well as community development funds."

"What for?"

"For Jorge, his wife and Daisy, the waitress. They're minorities. And the South Omaha area has redevelopment grants available."

"So," Rich took a sip of coffee. "What I want to know is how are we doing?"

"We lost money the first two months." Gisele pulled a spreadsheet from her case. She took a quick drink of coffee. "Let me correct that. We lost money big time in the first month. That was the renovation and opening...and really, to be expected. But month two we fell only a couple of points short. We were 10 points into the black last month. With the tax credits, development funds and some other business incentives I am applying for, we should do pretty well our first fiscal year."

"They've been asking about health care."

"With the new health care law we don't have to do anything until next year."

"They'll be disappointed."

"Tell them I'm looking into an affordable health care plan for them." Gisele broke off a small piece of bacon and fed it to Roommate. He snapped at it. "And take this back. It's a 401K plan. We can match between 7 and 15 percent."

Rich finished his coffee, stood. "They'll like that." He circled the counter.

"That's business. I can write this trip off now." A sly grin snuck between Gisele's cheeks. "Let's stay in bed for two days."

Rich stirred milk and sugar into his coffee and chuckled in the back of his throat. "I thought we were hiking the bluffs today, and touring the town tomorrow."

"I guess," Gisele sighed, putting plates into the sink. "Can Roomy come with us?"

"I think he should stay in his carrier."

"Okay."

Narrow dirt trails snaked north from the clearing into deep woods along the bluffs. Cool in the shade and humid, sunlight filtered through the high canopy of trees. Whirly bugs buzzed and birds flitted from tree to tree. Spots along the trail offered magnificent vistas of the wide Mississippi and wooded expanse of Illinois and Wisconsin. Tourist boats, riverboats and pleasure craft navigated the width of the dark green river. A tug pushed four barges heaping with black coal on down the river.

Something brown and low to the ground broke from the bushes ahead. Gisele jumped. The animal crossed the trail and disappeared in the scrub.

"What the fuck was that?" She latched onto Rich's arm.

"A bear."

"Like hell it was." Gisele slapped his shoulder.

"It was."

"What kind of wilderness guy are you?"

"A tenderfoot."

"Didn't you go to Boy Scout camp when you were young?"

"I did. The only thing I remember from camp is a kid that got his penis stuck in a Coke bottle."

Gisele stumbled, nearly collapsing in laughter. "He stuck his thing in a Coke bottle?"

"Things go better. Hey, it's not funny. It was seriously stuck. I bet that kid has a Coke bottle dangling from his dick to this very day."

Later they drove down to the Dubuque Port for dinner. An area of renovated warehouses and shops, they pulled into the small parking lot of a fading gray and green fake mountain chalet façade of the Europa Haus. The interior décor heightened the mock chalet effect, reminding Gisele of visits to Bavaria when she was young.

"My papa's brother, Andreas, would love this."

Rich peeked into the bar. Dark stained wood tables with walls festooned with small flags of many nations and pictures of 1930s alpine skiers and ornate mahogany bar ran the length of the opposite wall. A group of young people wearing Loras College t-shirts, huddled at a corner table, serious in their drinking. A large round belly, fleshy faced, blond crew cut, German looking bar man spread his blubbery arms wide. There was more to him than roly-poly.

"*Guten abend*!" he shouted. "Finally, our king and his queen have arrived!" He had cheeks like a baby's rosy bottom.

Rich and Gisele exchanged glances.

"Come, come," he waved both hands. "I have your Spaten cold and ready. And for the beautiful queen, I have a Reisling perfectly chilled."

Couples at a table laughed.

Reluctantly, Rich and Gisele approached the bar. With a flourish, the bar man produced a bottle of Spaten and foggy stemware glass of wine.

From aside his fat pink hand, he said to Rich: "Not to worry--I won't tell your wife you're stepping out with this gorgeous lady." He guffawed at his own joke, causing his large breasts to jiggle.

They sat, smiling.

"You ought to hire this guy."

"Just drinks tonight, folks, or dinner?"

"Dinner."

"I'll put your name in for a table. Your name?"

"Keeper." Rich tilted his glass and poured.

The bar man gave Rich a squinty look an instant, then waddled across the bar room into the dining room.

Gisele frowned. "Keeper, huh. Are we ever getting our lives back?"

Rich smiled sideways and drank.

Once seated Gisele marveled at the menu. "Beef Rouladen, Kassler Ribchen, Sauerbraten," she excitedly said. "Every meal with soup, red cabbage and spaetzle. Honey, you have to try the Beef Rouladen."

"I don't know. Everything is smothered in brown gravy. It looks too heavy for me."

"It's real stick-to-the-ribs food. You need some meat on your bones."

A dirty thought drifted across Rich's mind, but he kept silent, smiling at Gisele. "Okay, I'll try the beef."

"So," Gisele started after the waitress took their orders. "Other than not trusting the FBI guy, anything else about your meeting?"

"Not much more to tell. My contact with Omaha Police is a Detective Lieutenant named Lavender." Rich knew he needed to be selective in what he said to Gisele. "The FBI agent, Bertoloni says he has my back. I check in with both every couple of days. Not sure why Homeland Security wasn't brought in. Bertoloni seems to be handling my case singlehanded."

"And they don't know where the bastard that shot you is?"

"Yup." Her comment made his chest tighten. He scanned the people about the dining room. "And no idea who killed Bill More at the Daily."

"You told me that. Poor Edie. I'll call her when I get back."

The waitress placed plates before Gisele, then Rich. Gisele, as excited as a kid, dug right into her Sauerbraten. Rich spooned aside thick brown gravy and cautiously sampled his beef.

"Isn't this great?"

"Ummm, yeah," Rich replied. "It's good. How's yours?"

"Heavenly. I can already tell I won't be able to finish it."

Rich nodded, agreeing, chewing.

As they struggled out of the Europa Haus, carrying heavy 'doggie bags', Gisele held onto Rich's arm, groaning. "Owwww, baby. I think I ate too much. Can you drive?" She moaned getting into the passenger side of her car. She clutched her stomach all the way back to the cabin. "Oh, that was so good."

Roommate was overjoyed to be out of his carrier and doubly happy to be let out to pee. Later, the little dog voraciously chowed down on Gisele's leftover sauerbraten. Rich took a blanket, flutes and the second bottle of champagne out to the patio. "Come on, Gis."

"In a minute," she said from the bedroom.

Rich spread the blanket near the edge of the bluffs. He tied Roommate's leash to a nearby bush and worked the champagne cork.

Gisele opened the back door. Dressed in a sun dress, the inside light showed right through outlining her slim frame.

The cork popped and Rich poured, handing Gisele a flute as she crossed her bare legs and sat. A cloud of *Cashmere Mist* settled about her. The lights of Dubuque and along the river lit the banks.

"I wish every day could be like today."

"Me too."

"Do you?" Gisele gazed over the glass of bubbling amber. "Sometimes I wonder. You like running that bar. You like the people that work for you."

"I do."

"When all this bullshit is over will we have our lives back?"

"I hope so."

She reached over to his waist. "Will you stop carrying a gun?"

Rich hesitated. The moon, a silver half-slice, rode low in the eastern horizon.

"I knew it. You like carrying a gun."

"I don't...really." He pet Roommate absentmindedly. "You know how I feel about it. If you have a gun, eventually you're going to use it."

Gisele settled back. Rich turned on his elbow. He stroked her cheek with the back of his fingers. They kissed. Roommate loudly yawned. Gisele giggled. "We're boring the dog."

They lay silent, relaxed, comfortable, together. Rich kissed her again; it was so good to have her close. Gisele took his hand. She wasn't wearing any panties.

"Touch me, Rich. I miss your touch so much. You're gentle. You know where to touch me. I feel safe in your hands." Her eyes closed as her mouth parted; her hips lifted as her thighs tensed.

The sun shone bright and warm the next day, short sleeves weather, as Rich and Gisele toured the river walk and then drove into downtown Dubuque.

"It's rather drab," Gisele said, taking out a cigarette. "Looks a lot like the south side of Chicago."

"You have to smoke?"

"Hey, it's my car." She rolled down the passenger side window.

"This is definitely a workingman's town. South Side is a good analogy. Although, did you know in the eighties they had to import African Americans to Dubuque?"

"I didn't know that. I do like the older buildings. The church--St. Mary's was really cool. And that was a nice clock tower."

"I wanted to go to St. Raphael's but it's closed." Rich drove up 4th street and parked. "Want to take a cable car ride?"

"A what?" Gisele said, slamming the passenger door.

"This is Cable Car Square."

Rich reached out for Gisele's hand as they walked, admiring the old Victorian houses, shops and specialty stores. Families and couples ambled along the sidewalks of touristy Cable Car Square. Steep bluffs rose at the top of the street, Rich and Gisele stopped at the Fenelon Place elevator.

"I'll be damned." Gisele shielded her eyes from the sun and viewed the double tracks climbing up the bluff. "It is a cable car."

An overweight elderly pasty-faced woman with liver spots arching from temple to temple, sat in a narrow white-washed booth. Her nose lay buried in a romance novel. Rates were stenciled on the glass in cracked white paint.

"I'd like two round trip tickets."

"Thadah be six dollah," the old lady said, not looking up from her paperback. She snatched the ten-dollar bill Rich pushed forward and slapped four ones, two tickets and a sheet explaining the history of the Dubuque cable car. In large type, Rich and Gisele were instructed to enter the car, close the door and the operator at the top of the bluff would start the car.

The cars were built at a 45 degree angle, matching the incline of the bluff. Gisele climbed in and had to hang on to get to the back seat. Rich grappled up to the top seat.

"Is this damn thing safe?"

"Not like the Powell Street cable car we took on our honeymoon," Rich said.

Gisele squinted up. "Doesn't look like the Top of the Mark to me."

Rich read: "The cable car line was built so a local businessman could go home for lunch and not drive around the bluffs."

With a lurch the small car started upward. Squeaky, rickety, swaying, the car laboriously climbed. Halfway, the car passed a second car, on its way down. The people inside waved.

"They look terrified too," Gisele said under her breath.

"Where crooked little cars, climb nowhere near the stars."

KEEPER OF AN ORDINARY | 157

The nearer to the top the wider the vista, until close to the top a panoramic view of Dubuque, the Mississippi spread out behind them. The Julien Dubuque Bridge majestically crossed the river.

With a click, clack and a clunk, the car stopped. Rich opened the door and stepped out onto a deck and Tri-State views to the east.

"Shops or anything interesting up here?" Gisele asked, ducking her head exiting the odd-shaped car.

"Buy you an ice cream, little girl?"

"Mom told me I'm not supposed to talk to strangers. But you're cute. You'll do."

Leaning on the railing of the deck, they ate ice cream and idly looked out over Dubuque.

"Not a bad town."

"Uh huh." Gisele bit into her cone. "I'll pass on the t-shirt though."

Going back down the bluff, the remainder of the afternoon they browsed window displays and walked around Cable Car Square. That this was their last day together remained foremost in Rich's thoughts, but unspoken. They went into Shamrock Imports and looked around the Irish goods. They stopped, often, touching and stealing kisses, keeping as close to each other as they could. Rich watched Gisele with a pensive expression. She glanced over, smiling, her eyes shining.

"Okay if I smoke?"

"Go ahead. Where do you want to go for dinner?"

"I don't know." She turned her head away and blew smoke.

"There's a couple of places we could go. The casino has a restaurant."

"Might be fun to eat and gamble."

"I read a brochure about Town Clock Inn. It's said to have the best pizza in town, with a buffet and salad bar."

"Sounds okay to me."

"It's a funky place, in the basement of an office building."

"Charming."

"Or Dottie's Café. American food."

"Chicken fried steak, mashed potatoes, lumpy gravy and corn?" Gisele smirked.

"I'm counting on it."

Gisele dropped her cigarette to the sidewalk, crushed it, kicking the debris to the gutter. "Let's go." Something down the street caught her attention. She fixed on it, with narrow eyes.

"What is it, Hon?"

"Oh...nothing." She gave Rich half a smile, glancing back.

"Okay."

They parked in a side lot. The large sign dominated the front of the three-story gray brick and wood building that housed Dottie's Café. A square turret pointed upward from the building corner. This differentiated the café from similar structures in the neighborhood.

"Looks like a bar."

"Does, doesn't it." Rich held the glass door open for Gisele. "If the menu isn't to your liking, we can go have pizza."

The brown and cheddar cheese yellow diner featured a long counter and Formica tables with molded plastic chairs. A classic menu; though corned beef and cabbage with Guinness on tap seemed a nod to Dubuque's Irish heritage. Dottie's wait staff bustled about, prompt, cheerful and polite.

"This'll be fine," Gisele told Rich as she perused the laminated menu.

"Breakfast all day. I might have a Denver omelet."

"I'm thinking something light, like a Greek salad."

While they waited for their order, Rich reached across and took Gisele's hands in his. He smiled and studied her face. Her eyes fluttered and her lips pushed together. Tears glistened in the corners of Gisele's eyes.

"It's going to be really tough leaving you."

"I don't want to talk about it." A tear fell to Gisele's cheek.

Rich cleared his throat. "For as long as this situation goes on I'll make sure we see each other every two or three months."

"Promise me?" She wiped the tear from her cheek.

"Deal."

"And promise me you'll be careful."

"You needn't worry about that."

"I can't wait for this bullshit to be over."

They ate in virtual silence, almost too emotional to make eye contact. Lingering over coffee, Gisele started disengaging.

"You have the papers I gave you?"

"Yes."

"Okay, make sure you give those papers to your people."

"Will do." Rich nodded as they walked out. "Wow, look at that old car."

"And tell Tom..." Gisele halted. She spun about. A stricken look crossed her face.

An orange-colored customized fifties style four door sedan rumbled past. Rolling close to the pavement, it had a sweptback design with low roof, black tinted windows and fat white wall tires behind fender skirts. The front chrome grill and hood ornament gleamed in the low sunlight. The ornament resembled a running man.

"It's a Mercury."

A window rolled halfway down. George Jones' *White Lightning* blared out.

Mighty mighty pleasin'
Your pappy's corn squeezin'
Whew...white lightning...

Gisele's forehead creased above her nose as her eyes followed the car past Rich's shoulder.

A black tube stuck out the open window.

"Maybe it's Buddy Holly Days?" Rich wondered aloud. "They hold a memorial weekend in Clear Lake..."

"Richie, we have to go." Gisele urged him.

"That's in February..."

She grabbed for his arm. "Let's go. Now."

Fffffft...tink...ffffft...tink twice tapped the painted brick lintel above the entrance to Dottie's. Chips of stone fell, puffs of white dust drifted away from two small perfect holes.

Rich flinched and dropped to a crouch. His hand went to the .38 under his shirt. There were people all around. He ran with Gisele to the parking lot.

"Get in the car...quick."

They jumped into her Accord. Rich fired up the engine and scattered pedestrians as they squealed out of Dottie's lot. The Mercury had stopped down the street. Rich wheeled in the opposite direction and floored the accelerator.

"Gisele, what's going on?" He demanded above the engine noise.

"I've seen that car before." Her face twisted in fright.

"Where?"

"At the cable car place and just before we went in to eat."

"Buckle your seat belt," Rich yelled. In the rear view mirror, at the bottom of 5th street, he saw the orange Mercury stop and attempt a U-turn. A passing car blocked its turn. "Seeing the same damn car this morning doesn't mean anything." Rich loudly said. The Mercury burned rubber going down the street.

"I've seen it before that," Gisele confessed. "In Glencoe."

"Glencoe?"

"A couple of times. Do you think it's...?" Her eyes opened wide. "I don't see those bastards back there. You lost them."

"Oh, it's them and they're coming. They took a couple of shots at me." Rich knew they would take a parallel street to catch him. Driving with his left hand, he pulled his .38 from the holster. "Shit. If we'd taken my truck I have ammo in the console." Looking back, he said: "That car's a tank, even if the engine's customized there's too much traffic. It's wide and heavy."

"How'd they find us?"

Rich glanced at Gisele. "They must've followed you from Glencoe." He timed a stop light and sped through as the yellow flashed red.

She started hyperventilating. "I'm...sorry, Rich."

"Got to think" he muttered to himself. Another light turned yellow ahead. A car started turning left. Rich laid on the horn, speeding into the intersection. The other car hit its brakes. Jerking right then left around the car, Rich roared through the intersection. A tinny beep sounded behind. In the side mirror, Rich saw the driver's arm out the window giving him the finger.

"We could go to the police."

"No."

"They'll help us."

"Gisele," Rich slowed, looked both ways, then accelerated through a four way stop. "I haven't been completely honest. I don't trust the cops. A stack of hundred dollar bills and a night with one of Bratva's underage girls and the cops would give us up in a heartbeat." They reached the base of the bluffs and the end of 5th street.

"I think we lost them."

"No...not yet." Tires screeched as Rich swerved onto Bluff Street, racing south. He checked the mirrors. "We're lucky so far. They were in a bad spot and we got behind them. We've got some separation with the lights and traffic. It helps it's getting dark."

"Let's go back to the cabin and..."

"Can't...not right away."

"What are you doing?"

"I'm trying to lead them off the track. We need to head west, then north, east and come back to the cabin from the north. Gisele, get a map up on your phone, call out the turns."

Looking down 4th street Rich saw the Mercury accelerating to an intersection a couple blocks away. The stop light changed to red and the rush of cars forced the Mercury to jam on its brakes, skidding sideways.

Weaving in and out of traffic, Rich pushed the speed limit. "Keep an eye out for cops. I don't want to get stopped. If they have a police scanner they'll hear it."

They burned by St. Raphael Cathedral. Bluff Street ended with a long curving entrance ramp to the highway at Dodge Street, heading west. Rich pushed the gas pedal and the Accord downshifted as they banked right.

"Honey!"

A large semitrailer sped alongside them. Ahead the lane ended, merging. Rich had the accelerator to the floorboard with the Accord inching away. The truck driver sounded his air horn loud and long.

"Richie!" Gisele grabbed for the dashboard. Her phone fell to the floor.

His eyes flicked left across the mirrors, then forward. He gripped the steering wheel with grim determination. The double tires of the truck loomed closer and closer, towering over the Accord. The rusted guardrail neared.

"We're not going to make it."

Rich didn't back off, taking the lane all the way to its end, then bumping and lurching left onto Dodge inches from the Semi's front bumper. The shining chrome grill and oval red Peterbilt emblem filled the Accord's rear window. A scream of rubber and blue smoke burst from the truck's tires as the driver slammed on his brakes. They left the Semi behind as they rushed into the setting sun.

"Made it."

"God damn it. You've changed." Gisele raised her fist at him. "You're unpredictable. You take chances."

"Use your phone." He gave her a stern look. "Find me a northern route."

Gisele felt around and found her phone, then worked the map application.

Rich checked the rear view mirrors. He had the advantage of the sun now—they'd be looking right into it.

Confident he had given them the slip, Rich was less confident they didn't know where they were staying.

"Exit right onto Northwest Arterial," Gisele called out looking at her phone.

"Atta girl," He patted her knee, adding a grin.

"Stay on this for 10 miles. It becomes South John Deere Road. There's a turn to Peru Road."

"Don't tell me until we're close."

Northwest Arterial was a four-lane divided highway, with little traffic. Rich got the Accord up past 90 miles an hour. "Look for cops, Gis."

They sped north as the setting sun lit up the western sky a fiery red as banks of purple clouds boiled above. "Looks like the Gates of Hell," Rich thought.

"I'm worried about Roomy. What if those bastards..."

"Easy," Rich held his hand up. "We don't know that they know where we're staying." He squeezed her knee. "If we lose our heads, we'll make a mistake."

As it grew dark Rich saw no headlights trailing them for more than a couple of miles.

"This turns into South John Deere in a mile."

"Does it cross Peru Road?"

"No," Gisele studied the screen of her phone. "It's a right turn, sort of a switchback."

"We'll be approaching the cabin from the north?"

"Yes. Slow down...Peru Road is coming up fast."

A green road sign flashed in the Accord's headlights: Peru Road. Rich eased around the corner and onto the narrow blacktop through the thick woods.

"Look for parked cars. They might be waiting."

"Not much shoulder."

"Yeah." Rich grinned. Gisele got it. He shut off the headlights.

"What if they're there?"

"We'll find out."

A lone light strung over the road ahead glowed at the turnoff to the inn.

"Okay. I'm going to pull into the far parking lot. Then I'll go into the cabin and see if it's okay." He saw Gisele staring at him in the half light of the dashboard. "You're going back to Glencoe tonight. We can't stay here."

Rich stopped the car. He checked his .38. "I will signal you if it's all clear." He exhaled. "They don't want you...they want me, remember."

Gisele slid over to the driver's side as Rich stepped out. Crouching, with his revolver at the ready, he jogged across the lot. Dropping to a knee behind his truck parked in front of cabin 2, Rich ran his hand along the inside of the back and front bumpers, checking underneath. Nothing. That was good. Rich opened the cabin 4 door and flipped on the lights. Roommate woke in his carrier. He slipped into the bedroom, bath, opened the closet and peeked out the back door. He scanned the cabin. It didn't appear anything had been moved since they left that morning. Rich went and pulled the gun case from under the bed. He holstered the .38, unclipped it and exchanged it for the Glock. Slamming a mag into the Glock he pulled back and let the receiver load a round into the chamber. At the door, he waved to Gisele. She drove up and ran in. They held each other.

"You're shaking." Rich kissed her forehead.

"Never did I think this is what our lives would become."

"Me neither." He kissed her again. "I'm going to take Roomy out and check the back. You..." he paused. "You pack and...." Rich frowned. "...drive back to Glencoe."

"I don't want to leave you."

"Gisele, we have to split up."

"Maybe we're safe here?"

"I don't know if that's true. I don't know that they aren't parked in the shadows waiting for us to let our guard down. They could've been watching us for days."

"You've been right." Gisele reluctantly broke their embrace, going into the bedroom and throwing clothes and toiletries into her bag. "Damn it. Damn it." Rich got Roommate's leash and took him out.

Gisele had her bag on the counter, smoking, when Rich came back in. Roommate trotted up to her. "Roomy," she picked him up. "I'm going to miss you." The dog licked her chin and cheek. "You're such a sweetheart."

Rich packed and brought out his bags. "You have to go, now."

"I hate those bastards."

"I do too, honey. I love you, Gisele."

"I love you too." She ran water from the faucet, dousing her cigarette. "Love you too, Roomy." Gathering her bags she leaned over and kissed Rich, then Roommate.

"Text me when you get home." Rich switched off the interior lights and opened the door for her. "It might be a good idea to go to the Glencoe cops and tell them what's going on." He stood in the shadows, Glock up, watching as Gisele threw her bags into the back seat, slamming the door. She gave him a look, got in and started the car.

He watched her drive out of the lot and down the road. He wondered if she would be okay. As he turned away an engine started and a low riding car eased out of the blackness at the end of the road, following the red tail lights of the Accord.

Rich loaded up his truck. With Roommate under his arm he surveyed the cabin. There were beers and food in the refrigerator. He left the key and some dollar bills for housekeeping on the counter, then closed the door. Roommate took his spot on the passenger seat as Rich lay the Glock on the middle console and started the truck. He pulled the gearshift down to "R" and backed out, then pushed it forward to "D" driving fast through the lot, by the inn and to the intersection. The road was dark. He accelerated up the narrow lane, speeding north.

Chapter 10

Two hours out of Dubuque Rich's F-150 hurtled through the Iowa night westbound on Highway 30, retracing the route from two days prior. Twin headlights on high beam penetrated the dark road ahead. He had not seen another vehicle in many miles. Blackness, with only the red glow of his tail lights trailing, let Rich breathe easier.

The little black and white terrier snoozed on the passenger seat, undisturbed by The Clash *Spanish Bombs* playing low.

Rich battled weariness. He rubbed his eyes and scanned the dashboard gauges. Coffee the next time he stopped for gas might help. The emotional ups and downs of the past two days had exacted a toll.

A pin prick of white light winked in the dark behind, far behind, and showed in the rear view mirror. The light grew, separating into a pair of dots. The dots rapidly approached. Rich's eyes shifted from the road ahead to the beams in the mirror. His headlights picked out a road sign. A road crossed the highway. The dots became more distinct headlights, coming on fast. Rich checked his Glock on the console. He slowed and turned onto the road. Rough with loose gravel, the truck bounced. Rich swerved and spun the back end around, facing the highway. A cloud of dust drifted away. He switched off the headlights, unbuckled his seat belt and partly opened the door. He envisioned the orange Mercury pursuing him down the highway.

"I'm ready for you now." Rich, Glock in hand, clicked off the safety and slid low in the seat.

He heard engine noise before he saw the vehicle. Just as it passed the intersection, Rich snapped on his headlights.

A silver Jeep Cherokee sped through the glare.

He sat for a while, watching the red glow of the Cherokee's tail lights fade to the west. He had fully expected the Mercury. "Shit," he breathed. "I got to get a grip."

Rich pulled into a rest stop further down the highway. Semitrailer trucks were parked, with amber and red lights on, tucked in for the night. He tugged on his black White Sox hoodie, slipping the Glock into the front pocket, putting the leash on a sleepy Roommate and carrying him down. They walked across the lot to a dark grassy area. Roommate nosed around, peeing on a sign reading: Dog Owners Pick Up Waste. Cicada bugs buzzed in the night. A low watt bulb lit a small spot behind the brick restrooms. For miles beyond the rest area there seemed nothing but blackness. Rich pulled out the Glock and aimed into the black.

Blam...Blam...Blam...light flashed and brass casings spit out the receiver.

Silence and darkness enveloped Rich.

Roommate strained at the end of his leash, leaning away from Rich with large frightened eyes. Rich's ears rang. The stink of cordite drifted through the air. He pocketed the Glock.

"It's okay, Roomy."

The dog relaxed, yet remained tentative and cautious. The Cicadas started again.

"Come on," Rich gave a gentle tug on the leash. Roommate followed.

A heavyset trucker in thermal shirt and black jeans, wearing a beat-up ball cap, stood outside the entrance to the men's restroom. He stared with wary eyes as Rich and Roommate came out of the darkness.

Rich fixed him with steady eyes, a hand in his front pocket. "Evening," he said as he neared.

The trucker half stumbled with an awkward step back. "Ah, yeah, evening." He took another step, then turned and hurried across the parking lot.

Rich tied Roommate's leash to the faucet and stepped to the urinal. After, he doused his face and tried to dry on the hot air blower. He saw the heavyset trucker climb up to the cab of a semi as he and Roommate went back to Rich's truck. He filled water for Roommate and set the bowl on the floor of the truck. He locked the doors and dropped down the back of both seats. Picking up his phone he saw he missed a call from Gisele.

"Richie..." Gisele's voice quivered in the voice mail. "I had to stop for gas and...and as I pumped gas that big car, the orange one, pulled up next to me. I got scared. This skinny guy with greasy hair like Elvis and dressed in a long coat got out. Behind him some monster guy with shaved head, wearing a black tracksuit, gets out. This guy was all muscle, even his eyebrows had muscles. The skinny shit is suddenly in my face yelling. Gisele lowered her voice, mimicking: 'Var iz he?' I couldn't understand a word he said. He had this thick accent. 'Var iz he?' he's shouting. Who? That's all I could squeak out. 'Dot sun ah beach man you gots."

Rich clenched his teeth, taking in a breath.

"I didn't know what to say...he's...he's got his finger sticking in my face. The monster is right behind him. I'm thinking...there's mace in my purse in the car, that Taser thing in the glove box, a nail file on the dashboard and kitchen knife under the seat. I could take the gas nozzle and spray both these assholes then light a match. Then, then he says: 'he en Du-Bu-Key?' I said what? He said 'Du-Bu-Key...Du-Bu-Key. He en Du-Bu-Key?" Gisele let loose a shuddering breath. "I was so scared I got the giggles. I realized the skinny shit meant Dubuque. Were you in Dubuque?" She chuckled short. "Beep..."

The message ran out of time. "End of message. Next unheard message."

"When I lost it and laughed the monster guy got really pissed off. His face twisted up and he took a step toward me like he was going to grab me. I tried to pull the gas nozzle out of the tank, but it stuck. Just then an Illinois State Trooper drove into the gas station. They saw the trooper and moved back. He moved to Texas, I shouted. They looked at each other. 'I find...I keel,' the skinny shit said. I went in the convenience store and hung around near the state trooper."

Rich heard Gisele exhale and knew she was smoking. "I'm still shaking. I watched them drive off. Oh my god, Richie, it's getting worse. They're getting closer." She became quiet for a moment. "When the trooper left I got in my car and followed him back onto the freeway. Luckily he was driving east. I have to tell you, Richie. I thought you were being paranoid—but now I'm looking for that car everywhere. Oh, and I realized after I left Dubuque I forgot to give you some documents. I'm sorry. I can overnight mail them tomorrow. And I am going to Glencoe Police when I get to town. Richie, I miss you already. Those were two of the best days of my life. Love you. Be safe. Bye."

Rich clicked off voice mail and lay back in the seat. Staring out the windshield at the rest area, with small pools of pale yellow light and few other cars in the lot, Rich wondered, like Gisele, if this was how their lives would be from now on.

"Gisele, are you okay?"

"Damn, I'm glad you called. Yeah...yeah, I was shook up pretty bad. I'm all right now."

"Are they following you?"

"Actually, right now, there are no other cars behind me. I think they gave up."

"Maybe they've gone back to Du-Bu-Key?"

Gisele snorted. "Or on their way to Texas."

"You should've said Albuquerque."

"Hey--who is that skinny shit?"

"The monster guy is probably some muscle, but that's Nikolai Franko, also known as Nicky Franko."

"The guy that shot you?"

"The very same. And he took a couple of shots at us in Dubuque."

"If I had known that I would've stuck the gas nozzle up his scrawny ass and lit a match."

"I'd love to see that."

"He's a weird guy. I think he's nuts. Tries to look like Elvis and drives that old car."

"He's kooky, all right. A Teddy Boy...a Russian Teddy Boy. He wears drape coats, string ties, combs his hair in a waterfall, long sideboards, listens to rockabilly music and drives a customized car from the fifties."

"What's his deal anyway? Why the hell is he after us? Is it just because of those articles you wrote on sex trafficking?"

"Yes and no," Rich explained. "Nicky's mother is Suka. She worked her way up through the Russian mafia and now runs all the sex trafficking done by Bratva in the Midwest. I told you. My articles crippled them moneywise, as well as put a few key people in jail or got them deported. But I think they want my sources more than anything. I talked to a number of their people when they were being held in Cook County jail. They didn't hesitate to tell me everything. I think they thought it would help their cases. I'm pretty sure Suka, and Nicky, want to know who talked."

"You never answered me before, but why don't you give it to them?"

Rich exhaled. "Believe me, I thought about it. I kind of know Russians. It wouldn't have ended it."

"Yeah, I guess."

"Babe, be sure to stop at the Glencoe PD when you get home. Tell them the whole story. If they need to talk to me, get a number and I'll call them. You can tell them to contact Agent Paul Bertoloni, FBI Omaha."

"We're talking Glencoe—designer cops," Gisele added. "Oh, I'm sorry about those documents. I'll overnight them to you."

"Will you please get a carry permit? Gisele. I love you."

"Yeah...yeah...yeah...love you too."

Rich put both hands in the front pocket of his hoodie holding the warm Glock and settled in the seat. Roommate raised his head and eyed him with heavy lids. "Easy for you, Roomy." Rich patted the terrier's round head. He would try to get some sleep.

After sleeping on and off, Rich woke just as a misty gray dawn broke over the rest stop. Roommate fed and taken care of; a cup of bad coffee dribbled out a vending machine—and Rich took to the road. Omaha approached after a couple of hours on I-80. Exiting, Rich drove through the early morning deserted streets of South Omaha.

"Nobody out," Rich said to Roommate as they eased south on 16th Street.

Relieved, yet apprehensive, Rich spotted the red brick triangular outline and marquee of The Ordinary. The intersection appeared quiet. Rich passed The Ordinary and eased around the corner. Once assured there was no orange Mercury staked out on 16th or Vinton Street, he made a U-turn and drove to The Ordinary's rear parking area. He pressed the remote and the chain link gate slowly rolled back. Roommate had both paws on the dashboard, huffing happily watching the gate open.

The gate clanked closed behind as Rich stepped down from the truck, turning back to lower Roommate to the ground.

"We're home, Rooms."

The little dog sneezed and walked to the iron stairs. He paused to lift his leg on green moss edged brick foundation.

Rich gathered up his gear, tucking the Glock in the gun case, and climbed the stairs. Roommate jumped a stair at a time. He got left behind. Rich heard the dog whimper. He set his bags down on the landing and went back for Roommate.

Opening the door to the apartment, Rich set Roommate down and listened for a moment. The air hung still, stale and close. Roomy sniffed around. Rich brought his bags in and went to the pantry surveillance cameras. He opened the archives folder and checked two days prior. Cars in front changed in a blur, parking then driving off. He studied the cars, looking for the old Mercury. No, no Mercury or any other suspicious vehicles. He checked the back parking lot. The only movement was Jorge taking the day's trash to the dumpster. Rich clicked stop and backtracked on the recorded images. Tom and Daisy walked out together. Not unusual, although, they walked very slow and very close together.

Three bank envelopes of bar and restaurant receipts, and assorted mail, lay piled on the floor of the pantry. Rich picked up the mail and envelopes and dropped them on the table as he went through the living room to the bedroom.

Shaved, showered, a mug of hot coffee in hand, Rich sat at the table and booted up his laptop. He sorted through three days receipts and by the second cup of coffee had completely updated the bar's books. He ripped up junk mail and tossed it in the trash. Opening the dark web he emailed Gisele the spreadsheets, then put together a single envelope for the bank deposit. Curious, he searched among images of Mercury cars brought up by the search engine. Recognizable by the body style, the rust colored Mercury was a customized 1951 Mercury four-door sedan.

A noise, like a slamming door, sounded from the bar downstairs. Rich quietly put the bank bags in the gun safe and took out the sawed-off shotgun. He unlocked the dumb waiter door and climbed down the ladder to the bar below. A light shone from the kitchen. The bar was decorated with red pennants, white and red crepe paper streamers, cardboard helmets and large red flags with white N's. Rich crept to the doorway of the kitchen and, with shotgun at the ready, peered around the corner.

Jorge, his back to the door, busied himself preparing food.

"You're in early."

"*Ayyyyyyyy, meirda.*" Jorge spun around, grabbing his chest. "*Jefe!* Jew scared me." He saw the shotgun in Rich's hand. "Every ting *bueno*?"

"Oh, yeah." Rich glanced at the shotgun. "Didn't think anyone would be in yet. What's with all the decorations?"

"*Es* Husker game day."

"That's right. I forgot. What's on the menu?"

"Chili, *queso*'n' *pollo* wings'n' nachos." Jorge flashed a proud grin. "En brats wit sauerkraut or chili."

"Sounds good. Anything happen while I was gone? Any strange people in the bar?"

"*Nada, Jefe.*" Jorge shrugged. "How were days off?"

"Good, Jorge. I guess I'll leave you to it." Rich turned away and ducked behind the bar. He checked stores of bottled beer, wine and scanned the back wall of brown, green and clear liquor bottles. Tom had kept the service area well-stocked and spotless. Rich leaned the shotgun under the bar. The crumpled bag of fireworks from Jorge's grand opening debacle was now joined by a second bag. Rich opened and peered inside.

"Jorge?"

"*Si, Jefe?*" He stuck his head out the kitchen door.

"Did you buy more fireworks?"

His tone low, guilty: "*Si.*"

"We've got to get rid of these things."

"*Es mi* Carmelita's birthday next week. I take."

"See that you do." Rich searched the surveillance archives for the bar the previous days. Nothing unusual.

He checked the minutes left on his phone. He needed to go to a gas station and buy another burner phone soon. Rich keyed in Bertoloni's office number. It rang three times.

"This is agent Paul Bertoloni. I am away from my office. Please leave a message. Beep."

"Paul...this is...." Rich turned away from the kitchen door, not wanting Jorge to overhear. "Richard Rice. I had an incident in Dubuque when I was there with my wife for a couple of days." He walked to the end of the bar as he talked. "Nicky Franko must've followed my wife out of Chicago. He took a couple of shots at us. I lost him on the roads. He was driving an orange 1951 Mercury sedan. He confronted my wife at a gas station when she was driving back to Chicago. I don't think he knows I'm in Omaha. But I get a nagging feeling that things are heating up. I'll be ditching this phone. I'll call with my new number."

Rich clicked off his phone, head down, pinching his lower lip in thought. Not much Bertoloni can do with that information. At least he would be aware Franko has popped up and is on the move. Rich dialed his phone with his thumb.

"Lavender, here."

"Lieutenant. It's Richard Rice."

"Keeper. You going by your real name now?"

"No. I didn't think you'd recognize me."

"It's been more than a month. What's up?"

"I spent some time with my wife in Dubuque and she was followed out of Chicago by someone driving a '51 Mercury. I'm pretty sure it was Nicky Franko."

"No shit?"

"Yeah...no shit."

"A '51 Mercury, you don't see too many of them around."

Rich growled in the back of his throat.

"I'm kidding ya. You really think it was Franko?"

"Yeah...he took a couple of shots at us. Missed. I'm thinking things are starting to happen."

"Maybe." Lavender sounded distracted. "I'll ask for more drive-bys. And I'll stop in myself."

"I've got to get a new phone. I'll call you with the number."

"All right," Lavender said. "Keep me posted. And stay safe."

Rich pushed the END button on his phone, then ducked under the bar and crossed the bar room. "Jorge?" he called entering the kitchen. "I've got some errands to run..."

"*Jefe?*" Jorge exclaimed. "Can you go for enchiladas and salsa? I no think we got enough."

"Netti's?"

"*Si*, Netti's *es bueno.*"

"I like Jacoby's salsa."

Jorge shrugged, arms out, palms up. Rich nodded in reply and left the kitchen. "I tink maybe you like that skinny Maria at Jacoby's," he called after Rich.

"No, Jorge."

"No? I not so sure, *Senor* Keeper."

That Saturday The Ordinary was packed from the walls to ceiling with Husker football fans. Tom and Rich worked the bar nonstop from kickoff to the closing whistle, with but a short breather at halftime. Daisy made a couple of month's rent in tips alone as she weaved in and out of the tables to the kitchen, coming back with trays of nachos, enchiladas, wings or a brat or two. When it wasn't food, she was back and forth to the bar with beers. Jorge never left the kitchen. His wife Carmelita came in and lent a hand with the food prep. Rich caught sight of the whole crew working like a well-oiled machine. He couldn't deny the pride he felt. Gisele had pegged it, Rich thought as he tipped and pulled the handle for a draft beer. He and Tom were old friends, and he liked Daisy, Jorge and his family and especially, he liked The Ordinary.

Amid the bustle, shouts, laughter, clink of glasses, conversation, fizz of soda, Rich lost himself. With all the eyes on the game playing on the 72-inch HD TV, he tended bar with a grin. The aroma of food from the kitchen and smell of beer, mingled with perfume and cologne from the crowd. Groups of people, couples or solitary men standing in the corner, beer in hand, watched the game. The bar room, a riot of red and white decorations, melded with people and players on the screen. It liberated him from the fear; but not from work. Two drunks had to be cut off and asked to leave. They became belligerent, but a glance at Rich's .45 automatic in his shoulder holster made them compliant. Then the toilet in the Gents backed up. Some gal gulped down too much excitement too quickly and couldn't contain herself, giving it all back in a couple of splashes around the Ladies commode. Rich mopped and thought it amusing to be cleaning up puke with a .45 dangling below his arm pit.

Wild cheers broke out for a touchdown or great play from the Huskers. Silence fell over the room when Wisconsin, in white jerseys drove down the field to score. Anxiously, fans crossed fingers and concentrated as Nebraska worked down the field. They ran out of gas and downs at the 20 yard line. A field goal could win it. All eyes watched the kick, the ball turning over and over and just clearing the crossbar for the score. Wild cheers erupted as the local boys triumphed. Thank goodness there were no tall buildings, nor high cliffs, these fans took losses much too personally.

Hours after the game ended, and a scattered few stayed to continue drinking, Rich got everyone together.

"I've got good news," he said, as they wearily slumped in the far corner of the bar. "I met with the owner and got the numbers. We started out slow, but the last two months we've exceeded projections."

"So I won't have to look for another job?" Daisy said.

"Not unless you want one."

"Good, I like this one."

Tom laughed into his glass of club soda. "That's not what I heard when you were so busy you couldn't take a pee."

Daisy playfully bumped shoulders with him and smiled. "Shush, you."

"Hmmmm," Rich thought, recalling the image of Tom and Daisy caught by the surveillance camera out back. "I'll be quick," he glanced over at Jorge who had his head on his arm. "And before Jorge collapses. I'll meet with each individually over some of the things. And I know we talked about a health plan. Sorry, it's not going to happen. You'll have to sign up on the health exchange at least for this year. In lieu of a health plan I'm talking with the owner about compensating you for some of your costs."

"Sounds fair."

"I'm okay with that."

"*Si, es* cool."

"We're going to set up a 401K with matching funds...up to 10 percent."

"What's that?" Daisy wanted to know.

"We can talk about it later."

"I can fill her in," Tom volunteered. He and Daisy exchanged smiles.

"Hmmmm," Rich again thought. "That's about it. We've got The Ordinary off to a good start and in a sound financial position. We need to maintain that, and build on it. Tell all your friends and family, come on out. I want you all to know that you will benefit as much by The Ordinary's success as the owner." He made eye contact with Tom, Daisy and noticed Jorge's eyes closed. "You awake, Jorge?"

"*Ay, si, Jefe, si.*" His head popped up, a deep red mark across his cheek.

Gisele's overnight letter arrived a few days later. Rich held up the red and white cardboard envelope. It appeared as if it had been opened then reclosed with tape. Rich pulled out the documents and two letter sized envelopes. One envelope contained a handwritten note from Gisele explaining the documents enclosed and how much she missed him. The second envelope did not match the stationery. Rich ripped it open. Inside he pulled out a torn henna and blue note. He studied it—a 100 ruble bill. The engraving depicted a team of four horses rearing up. Bewildered a moment, Rich half laughed. Gisele played a joke on him.

"Hey," Gisele answered Rich's call.

"Honey, got the envelope with the documents and your note." He paused. "That was a funny joke."

"Glad you got the stuff. Joke? What're you talking about?"

"The 100 rubles."

"Rubles? I...still don't know what you're talking about."

"There was an envelope with a torn Russian bill."

"I didn't put that in the envelope. Russian?"

"Well, it was in a second envelope."

"That's strange. I have no idea how it got there. Wait. I remember two young girls behind me at the post office. Couldn't've been more than 13 and dressed kind of slutty. What kind of mother lets their daughter go out dressed like a hooker? They were really close behind me. I thought they were going to steal my purse. They talked and it sounded like Russian. They left when I did. No...they turned back."

"Maybe they mixed up their stuff with yours?"

"Don't know how. I'm certain I sealed the envelope."

Rich held up the envelope. "This has been opened and taped closed." He checked the front. "It's your handwriting on it."

"I don't know, babe."

"Me neither. Thanks for sending the stuff."

The call bothered Rich. He broke the phone into small bits, pocketing the SIM card and drove to a gas station to buy a new burner phone. Later in the afternoon he called Gisele to give her his new number.

"Where have you been?" She asked, anxious and talking fast. "I've been calling and calling."

"I got a new phone. Something happen?"

"The Russian money in the envelope bothered me. I went back to the post office..." Her voice raised a pitch, agitated.

"And?"

"I found the clerk that helped me. I asked him if someone had opened my overnight letter."

"What'd he say?"

"He said my daughters came back to put money in the envelope. Money I forgot to put in."

"Daughters?"

"Remember the two slutty girls behind me? The ones that talked Russian?"

"I remember."

"The clerk thought we were together. The girls came back to the counter and asked him for the envelope to put money in for their dad. He gave them my envelope, Richie." Her voice cracked.

Rich knew what this meant.

"He opened it and they put an envelope in."

"And they got my address from the overnight letter." Rich said nothing for a long time. Of course, Gisele knew what Nicky looked like. If she'd seen him, she would've run. When she went into the post office he had two of his girls follow her.

"Richie?"

For a moment, the bottom seemed to have fallen out of Rich's world and he was falling, falling. Although he realized, this had been inevitable.

"Richie?" Her voice wavered. "I..."

"It's okay, Gisele."

"But now they..."

"It doesn't mean anything, Gisele." He lied. "Did you go to the Glencoe Police?"

"I did, but..."

"Good." He cut her off. "Gisele, we'll be all right."

Chapter 11

Hoisting a case of clanking beer bottles up from the basement, Rich noticed Tom and Daisy walk in. They laughed with heads together, sharing a joke. Climbing out, Rich carried the box into the bar. Seeing Rich, Tom and Daisy separated.

"Hey guys," Rich said, ducking under the bar.

"Keeper."

"Boss."

Rich pulled open the case. "Tom," he said, restocking the bar cooler. "Can I talk to you for a minute?"

"Sure."

Daisy touched Tom's elbow. "I'm going to get ready for my shift." They shared a look, then both noticed Rich watching.

"You want to talk upstairs or here?"

Rich closed the cooler and picked up a manila folder next to the surveillance camera. He pitched the empty cardboard box toward the dumb waiter. "We can stay down here." Rich came out from behind the bar. "Take a seat at the table in the pool room."

"That special order came in." Tom sat as Rich pulled out a chair across from him. He noticed Tom had trimmed his square-cut beard. Neat and well-tended, it went down about three inches from his chin. Tom had also tidied up his appearance, wearing a clean gray polo shirt and jeans. His head freshly shaved, Tom looked sharp.

"You're spiffy today."

"I'm feeling good too."

"All right. Glad to hear it." Rich opened the folder and turned over some papers. "How's the program going?"

"Really good, Rich...ah," Tom checked over his shoulder. "Sorry, Keeper."

"Don't worry about it." Rich put a document before Tom. "Gisele got this from the state. It's a garnishment of your wages for past due child support."

"What? I've been paying."

"It's from before. You're three months behind."

"That can't be. I've paid this month, last month and the month before. Fuckers."

"It's that three month binge, before you got here." Rich tapped the paper. "My advice...keep paying a little more each month while they garnish your wages. You'll catch up."

"It just bites." Tom frowned. "Can't get ahead some times."

"No shit." Rich closed the folder and thoughtfully wiped his mouth and chin with his hand. "Still staying with your cousin down in Bellevue?"

"What?" Tom weakly smiled. "Yeah, she hasn't kicked me out yet."

Rich leaned back and folded his arms across his chest. His head cocked to the right, he regarded Tom silently. Tom fidgeted and stroked his beard.

"I called your cousin, Tom. She hasn't seen you in weeks. She said you've been spending time at Daisy's."

Tom's head fell back and he looked up to the ceiling. "Yeah...yeah. That's true. I didn't want to keep it from you...but..."

"We've been friends a long time, Tom. It's none of my business what you do in your off hours. I thought you were saving money and getting sober so you can go back to Seattle and try again with Laurie and your son Jimmy."

"I was going to tell you. We were just work pals at first. Then, something clicked." Tom swayed forward. "You know how you and Gisele seem made for each other. That's how it is with me and Daisy."

"How long have you two been serious?"

"About a month."

"Tom, I've got to be honest. If you're playing around with Daisy and planning to drop her and go back to Laurie, I'm going to be pissed off. I don't want to see Daisy hurt."

"No, no, it's not like that. Laurie doesn't want me. She told me that. She wants out. And I don't want to go back to her. I'm seeking joint custody for Jimmy, that's all."

Rich shook his head. "I'll take you at your word. Even though we're friends—I'm on Daisy's side."

"My track record is pretty bad."

"I'm on your side too. I think it would be great if you and Daisy got together. I think she is just what you need to straighten out your life."

"I didn't mean to put you in an awkward position."

"I know that." Rich hesitated. "But I have to put you in an awkward position with what I am going to tell you."

"What?" Tom expression became concerned.

Rich took a deep breath and tipped onto the back legs of his chair. "Remember I told you about the Russians out to get me..."

"Yeah...yeah. The ones that took a shot at you."

"Well, Gisele and I had a run-in with them in Dubuque. They didn't know my truck and followed Gisele back to Chicago. But..." Rich unfolded his arms and brought the chair forward. Hands on his knees, he breathed in and exhaled quickly. "They may know where I am now."

"What kind of problem are we talking about?" Tom wanted to know.

"Not sure."

"Do you know who?"

"A nut job named Nikolai Franko, Russian mafia." His lips tight, Rich nodded his head. "Franko drives a '51 Mercury like he's James Dean; and dresses like an English Teddy Boy."

"That's kind of odd." Tom absentmindedly ran his hand over his bald head. "Dangerous?"

"I would say yes...very."

"He got playmates?"

"Franko and a big boy cornered Gisele at a gas station when she was driving back to Chicago."

"Gisele okay?"

"A state trooper scared them off. It's me they want."

"Don't worry—we'll take care of them."

"I appreciate that, Tom. Seriously, just having you here helps. But...if it gets hot and you need to bail, I won't hold it against you."

"I'm not bailing. You haven't bailed on me."

"Thanks bud." They shook hands and broke into smiles. "Just make sure Daisy and Jorge are safe. That would be the best thing you could do."

"You guys going to do some work or chitchat all afternoon." Daisy stood, her arms folded and hip cocked.

Rich grinned at her. "I think we're done here. Thanks, Tom." He pushed back his chair and stood.

"Thank you, Keeper." Tom jumped up and grabbed Daisy whirling her around. She squealed through her laughter and tried to get loose.

Later that afternoon while Rich worked on his laptop upstairs, Tom called up the dumb waiter.

"Keeper?"

"Yes. What?" Rich minimized the screen on his computer.

"They just delivered an overnight letter for you."

Rich climbed down to the bar. Tom met him. He stood with a document-sized red and white envelope in his hand. They exchanged bewildered looks.

"What do you think it is?" Rich took the envelope.

"Look at the name and address."

Rich turned over the envelope and in the white address field, written in a very ornate hand, was: To: Richard Mr. Rice, The Ordinary and street address, Omaha, NE. It confused him a moment. He didn't recognize the handwriting. Circles above the lower case letter i seemed as if it was written by a child. "I better open this upstairs." Distracted, studying the envelope, Rich stepped onto the ladder in the dumbwaiter. "Thanks, Tom."

"You need me, I'm down here."

In his kitchen, Rich held the envelope up. The cardboard was too thick to see through. He shook the envelope. No sounds like powder or crystals gave any indication of its contents. He didn't trust opening the envelope by the draw tab. Rich pulled a long, thin bladed, wood handle filet knife from the stand by the stove. He walked into the living room. Roommate lay curled in a sleeping position on the couch. The dog lifted its head.

"Well, Rooms, if this envelope blows up in my face--it's been a blast."

Using the narrow blade, Rich slit along the top crease of the envelope. He peered in and pulled out a torn page from a newspaper. Circled in bold black ink was a one column story from the Chicago Tribune. The headline read: Daily Reporter Shot; In Critical Condition. The story had run after the attempt on Rich's life. He looked in the envelope, then checked the front. No return address and a postmark from the Chicago area left no doubt who sent the newspaper clipping.

Rich laid the envelope and knife on the table, pinching his lower lip, thoughtfully staring at the floor.

The phone buzzed. Rich didn't recognize the number, but it was a 402. "Yes?" He cleared his throat.

"Boss..." Daisy said. "Tom's got a bachelor party at the bar and we're swamped. He asked me to call and see if you can come down and help."

"Be right down."

"Thanks."

Rich looped the shoulder holster over his t-shirt and checked the .45 automatic magazine. He slipped on a gray and black checkered flannel shirt and went down the dumb waiter. Noisy, boisterous, laughing and talking, the bachelor party stood three deep at the bar. Rich checked in with Tom who was making 7 and 7's. "Thanks, man. We got three Heinies with tequila shots down there; two Coors and a couple of PBR draughts in the middle. A white wine for the guy in the black glasses (Tom and Rich shared a look of raised eyebrows.) and a ginger ale." He pointed.

"Tab?"

"The ginger ale."

Rich strode down the bar, clapping his hands. "We're going to get you guys all taken care of."

"Can we play pool?" one yelled.

"Hell yes." Rich popped the caps off three bottles of Heinken and set them in front of the three guys at the end. "Shots coming up."

"Play some music."

"What'd you want to hear?" Rich set out the Coors and draughts then lined up shot glasses.

"Got any rap?" A tall young guy yelled out, wearing an arrogant expression.

"Just old school."

"Old school?"

"Beasties, Run DMC, Tone-Loc, Grandmaster Flash, like that." Rich poured *1800* tequila from a bottle over the line of shot glasses.

"Put it on."

He stepped over to the music computer and opened the rap music folder. "Tell me if you like this one."

From the speakers blasted: *"I like big butts..."* A loud whoop went up and the bar room erupted in a sing-a-long.

Drink orders filled, Rich went up to the ginger ale guy. "You're tab, right?"

"I am. Sorry, we're bar hopping." He sipped his fizzy drink. "We've got a limo coming in an hour."

Daisy set out chips and salsa, peanuts and popcorn on the bar and tables. She escaped the clutches of a drunk partier diving to grab her backside as she walked by.

"Tell your pal to leave my waitress alone."

"That's the groom."

"Congratulate him for me." Rich leaned over the bar, talking into ginger ale's ear. "Cash or card?"

"Card."

"Mind if I run it now?"

"No problem." He put down his ginger ale and pulled out his wallet from an inside pocket of his sports jacket. He handed Rich his credit card.

"Thanks." Rich turned to Tom. "Everything on the tab?"

"Add two whiskey sours."

"Hey," Tom shouted over the tumult. "Remember your bachelor party?"

"I do. Nirvana and Dinosaur Jr. at the Melody Ballroom the June before *Teen Spirit* was released."

"Too many *Henrys*."

"Damn straight. You had me almost convinced Gisele was leaving me at the altar and running off to Mexico with you."

Tom laughed. "Too many *Henrys*."

An hour later the bachelor party noisily spilled out of the bar and poured into a limo parked out front.

"Hey, man...this place is awesome. We'll be back."

Panic seized Tom a moment. "Where's ginger ale guy?"

"Don't worry. I ran his card before." Rich said. "We got his number."

But the last man out was ginger ale and he stopped to settle up.

"You be careful." Rich waved as he left.

Daisy stood at the bar, arms akimbo, eyes narrow and mouth pulled tight. She glared at Rich.

"What?"

"Of all the songs in your computer you had to play *that* song."

Rich replied with a chuckle and a wink.

The next day moved slowly, with Tom working on a faulty keg line in the basement, Jorge prepping food in the kitchen and Rich cutting limes and checking stocks behind the bar. A couple and a solo were at tables. A short, stocky man with close cropped blond hair, wearing a beige suit, came in.

Style Council's *Big Boss Groove* played low over the speakers.

"What's good for lunch, Keeper?"

Rich glanced over. "Hey, Lieutenant." They shook hands over the bar. "Pretty much whatever's on the menu. Grab a seat; I'll be over in a sec."

"Sounds good." Lavender surveyed the room and went to a round table in the corner next to the big screen television. He pulled out a chair ensuring his back would be to the wall.

Rich came up with a menu. Jorge passed behind with plates of sandwiches for the couple. He caught sight of Lavender and did a double take.

Handing the lieutenant the menu, Rich sat. "Have you talked to Bertoloni recently?"

"Yeah...just yesterday. I usually talk to him a couple times a week." Lavender squinted through his black rim glasses, finally taking them off. "I can see better without my glasses sometimes."

"I wonder if he's ducking my calls. I haven't talked to him in a couple of weeks."

"Busy guy."

"I guess. I'm sure Nicky Franko knows where I am."

"*Hola*, Sergeant," Jorge said, coming up to the table.

"It's Detective Lieutenant now, Jorge." Lavender tilted his head and scrutinized the Hispanic. "Been leaving the parked cars...parked?"

"Don't be busting Jorge's chops," Rich said, without rancor. "I'll make you pay for your meal."

"*Ayyyy, perdon*, Lieutenant. I walk straight now."

"We've both come up in the world."

The two men exchanged faint smiles.

"I'm just needling you, *amigo*." Lavender took a quick glance up and down the menu.

"What you like?"

"I'm thinking a couple of tacos would do me fine."

"*Si*, no *problemo*."

"A beef taco and chicken taco. Some beans and rice would be all right."

"*Si, gracias*."

"Thanks, Jorge."

"You want a beer with that?" Rich put in.

"Naw...a coffee, Jorge."

"*Si*," Jorge said, taking the menu and disappearing into the kitchen.

"If you talk to Bertoloni tell him I'd like a call." Chair legs barked on the floor as Rich stood. "I've got to get back behind the bar."

Tom climbed up from the basement. "Try that new line," he said ducking under the bar.

Rich reached down for a glass.

The door opened. A group entered.

A hand slapped hard on the bar. Rich looked up. A crude blue-black tattoo *OMYT* crossed the back of a small bony hand. The hand lifted, revealing a torn 100 ruble note on the polished mahogany. The torn half showed a statue of Apollo, in a chariot. From his shirt pocket Rich picked out the torn ruble sent him, an etching of a team of horses. He nudged the bill forward. The ripped edges matched.

"I been finding you," Nikolai Franko said, in a heavy Russian accent.

"I've been expecting you."

He had tiny brown eyes set deep in the hollows of his long bony face. His features were so narrow there seemed to be a fold running from the bridge of his hawk-like nose to the crown of his forehead.

"'Specting me?" Nicky laughed in a queer wheezy manner. His mouth opened wide while his pink tongue stuck out stiff. Rich then understood why they said Nicky laughed like a snake.

His hair, the color of oxblood leather, had been teased and greased up to a bouffant atop his compressed head. A waterfall of bouncy glistening strands spilled over his forehead while a curl pointed out the rear.

A couple paces back from Nicky's right stood a large, well-muscled behemoth in a black tracksuit under a long black leather coat. From his shaved head and round, rippled face, Rich figured this was the monster who had accosted Gisele. Lounging by the door Rich noted Dedmon. He couldn't say it caught him by surprise. Chewing gum, Dedmon arrogantly beamed and gave Rich a one finger salute.

Between Nicky and the jumbo stood a heavily made-up petite young girl no more than 12 or 13 years old. Her hair, the color of white satin sheets, hung long, with uncoiled ringlets about her face. She had the broad forehead, tumescent nose and pointed chin of Eastern European descent. Her skin, an alabaster tone, accentuated her big round blue eyes. She had a skinny shape with all her points and bumps barely concealed by a flimsy silver shift. Narrow angular legs, without stockings, extended from a hemline just below her sex. She sucked the end of her thumb, eyed the men and swayed her hips side to side.

Rich pulled his lips tight and down, disdainful like a parent. He looked away. Tom's face, however, was a moving confession of confusion. His eyes devoured the girl then seemed to draw back in a kind of self-loathing.

She knew her business and skipped over Rich and played for Tom's attention.

While pleasing the eye, the girl gave only displeasure to the nose. A volatile mix of scents wafted about her; cheap schoolgirl perfume, spunk, hair spray and an overwhelming sharp reek of perspiration and urine. "Stripper sweat," thought Rich.

All men looked at her, except Rich and Nicky. Neither took his eyes off the other.

"Yes, expecting you." Rich squinted at the shorter, slight framed man. "I've got something for you."

"You damn god right you got sum'thin' for me." Nicky's hand went inside his coat, to the butt of a revolver tucked in the waistband of his peg pants. "You steal million dollar from my pocket with your newspaper lies."

"She can't be in here."

"Irina can, I say okay. She drink you under table."

"I'm sure her family is quite proud. Where you from, Sis?"

"Maribor...Slovenia."

"We have laws. Get her out of here."

Nicky spoke into the ringlets over her ear. He smacked her round butt hard as she turned and sent her awkwardly forward. She let out a "whoop" and faked a playful smile. But it hurt. Nicky sniggered dirtily. Hungry eyes followed her small, firm backside beneath the shimmering shift. Irina reeled in the men as she went past Dedmon and out the door.

"That was supposed to be my daughter?" Rich asked.

"I clever, *da*?" Nicky squinted, opened his mouth and stuck out his tongue, but did not laugh. "We follow...we follow you wife. We get lucky. She go post office. Maybe I say she send you love letter. Irina, she smart. She and girlfriend say they daughter, get address."

Rich looked past Nicky. "Bar's closed folks. Please leave immediately." The couple at the table paused in the middle of eating, confused.

"Jorge?"

"*Si, Jefe*," Jorge shouted from the kitchen.

"Come here and show these people out the back door."

"I can do it," Tom said.

"I need you right there, Tom."

"*Que?*"

"*Dejar rapida*, Jorge. Don't worry about your bill, folks, just leave."

The time had come. Rich fought a hollow sensation in his belly and almost laughed recalling Gisele's spot-on imitation of Nicky's thick accent and mangled English.

"Dees way." Jorge waved, shrugging his shoulders, saying "ah dunno" as he escorted the couple through the kitchen.

"Wot 'bout him, dere?" Nicky jerked his head in the direction of Lt. Lavender.

Staring nonchalantly out the window, Lavender talked on his cell phone.

"He's waiting on his tacos."

From the cooler under the bar Rich brought out a green liter bottle. He jerked off the cap and turned the bottle toward Nicky. He pointed to the white label with its charging grizzlies.

"Hey, Yuri," Nicky breathed. "Beer is *Three Bear*."

His eyes and mouth parted in surprise, the big guy stepped forward. His voice rumbled from the depths of his belly: "Is not?" He had an air about him, like damp earth or someone who didn't tidy up after shitting. The two exchanged quick Russian.

"Yuri'n me, we want know where you get *Taranov Three Bear*?"

Rich moved the shot gun to within reach, then set out two hourglass pilsner glasses and started to pour. The bottle shook in his hand. He heard Nicky's windy giggle as he pushed the glasses forward.

"*Amerikanskaya Piz'da*."

"What does that mean?" Rich wanted to know.

"American pussy."

Rich glowered in reply. He drew in a deep breath, let it out slow, and the butterflies in his belly landed.

Nicky thumbed over to Dedmon: "No beer *vor* bull?"

"He can pound sand. I don't know if he likes Russian beer or American beer. I know he's had an ace up his sleeve all this time."

"What that mean?"

Rich shrugged then exchanged a look with Tom. Tom turned his hand palm up. Rich gave him a quick nod.

"*Spasibo*, dead man." Nicky and Yuri clinked glasses. "Beer patrol." They tilted back and drank.

Kitted out in a stylized fifties era Teddy Boy outfit, with ruffled white shirt and string tie, Nicky's powder blue drape coat hung off his shoulders as from a wire coat hanger. He seemed in constant motion, all twitchy and darting eyes.

"Some music now?"

"Shostakovitch?"

"*Nyet*...dumb ass...rock ah roll."

At the computer Rich scrolled the music titles. He took a quick look at the surveillance camera. Nicky's Mercury was parked out front. Police cars arrived, blocking Vinton Street. In the background Johnny Burnette Trio's *Train Kept A'Rollin* played.

"*Da*, yeah. We talk?"

"Talk?"

"I like you. Maybe I let you leef." Nicky shouted over the music as his quiff shook and head bopped in a haughty manner. "You geef me names...and you geef me..." His arms waved around. "...Deez. I let you go."

"Fuck you, Nicky." Rich spat. "You get nothing and like it."

"Maybe I take when I done wid you." Nicky laughed into his beer.

"You'll never get the names."

Dedmon stepped forward. "Listen to reason, Mr. Rice."

Out the window Rich noticed a SWAT team setting up on the rooftop of the garage across the street.

Lavender saw them as well and jumped up, pulling out his side arm. "All right, you three...Omaha Police--put your hands on the bar."

Nicky, Yuri and Dedmon turned on Lavender.

"Tom!" Rich hissed. He underhanded his .38 to him. "Take out the big guy."

From inside his leather coat, Yuri brought out an AK 74 with sawed off stock and extended drum magazine. He fired from the hip, riddling Lavender, whose body twitched and jerked against the wall as blood spit out a line of red holes down his chest.

"Ballet Kalashnikov," chuckled the small Russian.

Pop...Pop...Pop.... Tom fired the revolver at Yuri, hitting him at least twice in the right shoulder, spinning him around.

Nicky dived backward, turning over a table for protection. He pulled a long barrel .357 from his belt.

Rich flipped up the shot gun from under the bar. In one motion he cocked it and blasted Dedmon square in the belly. Not once, but twice Rich hit Dedmon, folding him forward and sending him reeling back. His face looked like he walked into a surprise birthday party—except someone had already blown out the candles on his cake. His yellow shirt went red, a wet tattered mess as he crumpled by the door.

Turning back, Yuri sprayed the bar.

Rich ducked, covering his head. Bullets shattered the mirror behind the bar. Glass crashed. Bottles of brown, green and clear glass exploded alcohol along the shelf. A tap got blown off and a geyser of beer sprayed to the ceiling. Shards of glass and wood splinters ripped through the air. Booze splashed all around Rich. He grabbed a cocktail napkin floating in the air, tore it in half and stuffed paper wads into his ears. Glass stung his arm like shrapnel, and liquor drenched him.

Tom rose up, shooting at Yuri. "You bastard."

The monster stitched Tom up one side and down the other. He was dead before he dropped. Rich, his arm shielding his eyes from flying glass, saw Tom in a heap, blood all over his body. The side of Tom's head had been shot away, gray globs of brains oozed, a white eyeball and blood drooled down his beard and shoulder. The good side of his face appeared serene.

Yuri emptied the magazine then silence and smoke filled the bar.

A large triangle of broken mirror let Rich see over the bar into the room. He noted Yuri favoring his shoulder as he lowered himself behind an overturned table.

Someone groaned.

Yuri breathed hard, like a sob.

Nicky yelled at him in Russian. "*Oyobuk.*"

Shot up, Yuri clumsily changed magazines.

Rich jumped up. *Boom...Boom...Boom.* He blew off a corner of the table Nicky hid behind, and put a hole in the wall above Yuri.

"You no can win."

Squatting down, Rich reloaded the shot gun from a box of shells under the bar. He saw the bags of fireworks left by Jorge. Opening the bag he spilled out a pile of firecrackers, sky rockets, aerial and barrel bombs. The shot gun across his legs, he picked up five red barrel bombs. Taking a lighter from the debris, he lit the fuses.

Sirens pulsed outside, coming.

"I din not finish da beer," Nicky yelled.

"Coming up." Rich lofted the fizzing fistful over the bar.

Bang-bang-bang-bang-bang.

"There's your beer, asshole."

Pow...Pow...Pow...Pow. Nicky shot holes along the front of the bar. Splintering wood hit Rich. Light shone through the holes.

Rich pushed assorted fireworks into the paper bag, twisted the top tight and lit it. He heaved the flaming bag across the bar room. Rockets whistled and zipped across the room with sparks flying behind. Whines and screams, snapping firecrackers and billowing smoke filled the bar.

Ka-Blam...an aerial bomb went off. The concussion shook glass from the shelf.

Rich's eyes burned and watered; he coughed from the smoke.

Hoy Hoy Hoy by the Collins Kids blared through the speakers.

A cartwheeling, sparking rocket ricocheted behind the bar. He covered up, but the flaming missile set Rich's shirt on fire. He beat out the flames.

Again Nicky yelled in Russian at Yuri. It sounded like the big man whined.

A loudspeaker crackled from the street outside.

"You in the building...this is the Omaha Police. We have the building surrounded. Come out with..."

Nicky shot through the window, shattering the glass.

Rich took a chance and blasted the shot gun through the haze where he could vaguely see Nicky standing.

Yuri squeezed off a line of shots along the ceiling above the bar.

Rich hunkered low. "I just replaced that window." He brushed broken glass off his shirt.

"I take from you pay when I own."

The lull allowed Rich to take stock. He checked the box of shot gun shells. One shell left. He loaded it. He had the .45 in his shoulder holster, but only an eight round magazine. He looked at Tom and couldn't see what happened to the .38. Seeing his friend dead angered Rich. He remembered his dad telling him the cool head prevails. He struggled to maintain an even temper, knowing if he gave in to the rage, he'd make a mistake and be killed. That wasn't going to happen. But, he had to get upstairs somehow, for his Glock and more ammo.

Scanning the fragments of mirror on the wall, Rich saw through the smoke Nicky gesturing with his arm. Yuri moaned as he raised up to a knee.

Rich emptied the shot gun into the smoky corner. The table protecting Yuri blew up into sharp bits of wood, though he dropped down, eluding a full charge of buckshot. The shot gun was done. Rich eased out the .45, listening through the pounding of his heart.

Grunting, Yuri stood and firing the AK 74 from his hip, charged across the room.

Rich noticed the movement in the mirror pieces. He pulled back the receiver of the .45, ready.

The big man jumped on his back, intending to roll off the bar and land on his feet behind. Strewn with broken glass and pools of beer and alcohol the polished top was too slick. Yuri's leather coat slid him off the bar. He came down hard, the small of his back landing on the jagged bottom of a broken whisky bottle.

"Ahhhhhhhhhhhh," Yuri screamed, writhing no more than a few feet from Rich.

Rich grabbed the hot smoking barrel of the AK 74, wresting it from Yuri's grasp. Holstering his .45, he turned the AK around. Careful not to nick the femoral artery, he put two quick shots to the outside of Yuri's left thigh and added more rounds into his right thigh. The monster's large body convulsed with the impact of the bullets. Blood seeped out the holes. "That's for Tom," Rich whispered through clenched teeth. He put three more slugs point blank into Yuri's left shoulder. Blood splattered Rich's face. "I'm going to keep you alive. You've got a date with ol' Sparky." Wiping away the blood from his face, Rich rose up and emptied the AK's magazine at the table where Nicky cowered. Then he hurled the useless submachine gun at him.

"Yuri? Yuri?"

The big Russian whimpered.

"You son bitch!" Nicky let loose with his revolver, sending chunks of wood flying.

A large spinning chip of glass caught Rich, tearing a swatch of shirt and flesh from his left bicep. He grimaced, biting his lower lip. Slowly, he picked the baseball-sized piece of glass out of his arm. Blood dribbled out the jagged hole. The wound burned. Rich noticed a second bag of fireworks. He lit it and lobbed the flaming bag.

"You crazy."

The bag bounced off the overturned table and rockets and firecrackers began exploding.

A flaming rocket hit the computer under the bar. Primal Scream's *Rocks* blasted out the speakers.

Rich reached up and blindly shot off four shots from his .45. He crawled and crouched, slipping on spent shells and crunching glass as he moved to the end of the bar.

A sparking pinwheel ignited a puddle of alcohol.

Nicky replied with a couple of shots. "I keel you now."

Staccato bursts of firecrackers and quick white flashes filled the room. Rich broke from the bar to the dumb waiter in the back. Glancing over, he caught a glimpse of Lavender slumped in the chair. His beige suit striped with blood, Lavender managed to slightly move his head and blink.

"Where you run?"

Rich shot back, knowing he had but one bullet left. He picked the bloody wads of paper out of his ears and with his good arm gripped a high rung and climbed.

"Rup...Rup...Rup," Roommate barked at the top.

"Roomy, get out of the way." Breathless, Rich scrambled to the second floor. The small terrier excitedly ran back and forth, yapping. "Get in the bedroom, boy."

"I come for you."

Impulsively, Rich shot down the dumb waiter. The .45 automatic was empty. Holding his bleeding arm, Rich staggered across the kitchen. He reached the gun safe and spun the combination. His hand trembled.

Out the window Rich saw Omaha Police huddled on the rooftop of the garage across the street. He heard a helicopter overhead. Sirens filled the air.

"What dez?" Nicky's voice echoed from the dumb waiter.

"Rup...Rup..." Roommate barked at the pantry door.

"Nice doggie."

Rich jerked down the lever and pulled the heavy door back. He tossed the .45 in and grabbed for his Glock. A noise came from the pantry. He shot twice around the door.

"Is close...no cigarette," Nicky laughed, wheezing.

Two more shots and Rich heard Nicky grunt and curse softly. "You *zhopa*."

He answered with three rounds in rapid succession.

Rich leaned away as bullets splintered the door jamb.

"Rup...Rup...Rup...Rup."

Taking careful aim, Rich squeezed off a shot, only to have the Glock's receiver lock open. He realized instantly he hadn't changed magazines since the night at the rest stop.

Nicky heard the receiver lock and leaped from the pantry. The right sleeve of his blue coat was soaked red. His greased up hair flew wildly about his head. His frenetic eyes blazed. Red buckshot dots speckled the side of his narrow face. He sprinted from the kitchen and caught Rich as he turned back to the gun safe.

Rich got slammed hard against the safe as something hit him in the back of his head. Dazed, he turned and landed a right fist into Nicky's face. The Russian stumbled backward and fell on his butt. Rich kicked the revolver out of Nicky's hand. It clanked and spun across the wood floor. Nicky slapped at Rich's foot and clamored to his feet. Rich grabbed his wrist and pulled him to the floor. Struggling up, Nicky grabbed a chair and raised it over his head. He brought the chair down on Rich's shoulders, sending him crashing onto the table. The table legs gave way. Laptop, papers, books scattered all over the floor.

"Rup...Rup...Rup."

"Shut doggie up." Nicky shouted, enraged. He kicked at Roommate. The little dog dodged and rolled away.

Groggy, Rich managed to get up on his knees.

Nicky skipped forward. The thick crepe soles of his blue suede Brothel Creepers caught Rich under the chin, jerking his head back. White light blinded him. Something in his mouth tasted salty--his own blood. The back of his head ached. His sight slowly cleared. He found himself on his back.

Casually, Nicky picked up his .357, flipping open the cylinder and reloading. He went to the window.

Red laser dots swam over the ceiling and along the walls.

"You in the window. Come out of the…"

Laughing like a viper, Nicky opened the window and squeezed off three quick shots at the snipers on the rooftop.

"You miss show. Cops in barricade. Helicopter. Fire engines, Snipers on roof. Is like circus."

Rich shook his head, trying to regain his senses. "How are you going to get out of this, Nicky?"

"How I get out? Is simple. I geef up."

"What?"

"*Da*, I geef up and go jail." He huffed a giggle. "Then I get deported. Is free ticket home." He stood over Rich.

Keep him talking, Rich thought as he slowly came around.

"I get deported, go home. Russians make big show. For big show I taken in cuffs to prison. TV see me go in front door. It look bad for Nicky." He paused, breaking into a twisted smile. "TV no show me walk out back door prison. My Mercedes wait. I get in, drive off, free man. Ha!" He snapped his fingers. Flaring his elbows out, Nicky did a jaunty little walking dance.

Rich attempted to get up.

"I toe you, I get everything. Russian proverb say: Little thieves are hanged; but great thieves escape."

"Thief? Don't flatter yourself. You give thieves a bad name. You're a pimp. You buy and sell human beings."

"And you no understand world. I geef service. Only thing man want is the money and da pussy."

Rich squeezed his eyes together, rapidly blinking.

Nicky massaged his bloody arm. "You get me good…but I win." He took a cell phone out of his pocket.

"For Suka, my mama. You lucky. You keel me. My mama keel you wife."

"And the names?" Rich spotted the opened overnight letter and filet knife among the debris from the overturned table.

"I geef shit. I keel you, they shut up. I miss you before. Why you moof?" He held his phone up. "Smile. Say the cheese." Nicky snapped a picture. "I text mama now." Looking down, he thumbed a text.

"Rrrrup." Roommate dashed from the corner of the living room. The dog leaped and sunk his teeth into Nicky's ankle.

"Aaaaaaaaarrrrrrr, *Svoloch*," the Russian shrieked, hopping and trying to shake Roommate off his leg. He dropped the .357 and grabbed for the black and white dog.

Taking a deep breath, Rich seized the wood handle of the filet knife.

Nicky gripped Roommate by the nape of the dog's neck. Screaming from pain he tore the dog off his ankle. "You the fuck doggie."

Roommate writhed in Nicky's grasp, growling and snapping his teeth.

Nicky raised his arm high and came down fast, like cracking a whip.

"Rup..." The terrier went limp in Nicky's hand, its neck broken.

He flung Roommate's dead body, chuckling as it tumbled to the wall.

"Dat shut doggie up."

Anger surged through Rich. He half rose and plunged the filet knife into the side of Nicky's knee. The blade stuck a moment, then slid all the way through.

Nicky yelled, his face contorted as he frantically reached for the knife. His leg went straight and he tipped over, flopping around. The phone clattered to the floor.

"You motherfucker," Rich spat out. Finding his feet, he stood, hands on knees, pulling in his breathe. He picked up Nicky's .357.

"Pull out knife. Pull out knife. I let you leef."

"No way." Rich took aim at the center of Nicky's chest.

"Go do. Go do. You Americans are weak like girl. You not...." He reached up and grabbed the long barrel, pulling the revolver to him.

Blam. The muzzle flash singed Nicky's shirt. Rich smelled burnt meat and cotton.

A fountain of thick blood spurted from Nicky's chest. It gurgled out his mouth as his back arched. The fountain turned to a river down the ruffles of Nicky's shirt front. Air from his lungs bubbled up bloody from the wound. His mouth moved as he tried to talk. His hands clawed at his chest as a red pool spread beneath him. Nicky's narrow face turned ashen. The bony body relaxed. Nicky's eyes glazed over staring vacantly. His tongue stuck out his open mouth.

"You even died like a snake."

Not for more than an instant did Rich regret. He wiped off the .357 with his shirt tail and placed it in Nicky's limp hand. He went to the gun safe, took a loaded magazine and changed out the Glock. Red laser dots followed him. He carefully picked up Roommate's limp body and laid him on his cushion on the couch. He arranged the small dog as if sleeping. He murmured: "I'm sorry, Rooms."

The screen on Nicky's phone showed a photo of Rich, laying as if dead. A text box message written in Russian had not been sent. Rich clicked SEND and received a notification. That bought him some time.

He rifled through Nicky's pockets, finding a ring of keys.

At the window red dots circled on Rich's chest. He shouted through the window. "Get an ambulance. There are wounded."

Rummaging through the gun safe Rich tucked extra magazines and ammo for the Glock and Springfield rifle into a nylon drawstring sack. He quickly oiled a cloth patch and pushed it down the barrel of the Glock. He holstered the Glock and took out the rifle. With the bolt open, Rich angled his thumbnail and peered down the barrel. It gleamed. He thought: Dad taught me how to shoot with this rifle.

"I'll be coming out the front door."

Rich climbed down the dumb waiter. Layers of smoke drifted through the bar room. It smelled of alcohol, charred wood, cordite and the sweet sickly stink of blood. A small blaze burned on the floor. Rich stamped it out. He stepped over chairs and around a table to Lavender. His complexion looked like parchment. He'd lost a lot of blood, but his eyes followed Rich.

"Lieutenant?"

Lavender blinked.

"There's an ambulance coming. You've got to hang on."

His bluish lips trembled.

"You're going to be okay."

A flicker of light filled Lavender's eyes.

"Hey, we won."

Rich walked through busted up tables and chairs, broken glass, wood shards, brass shell casings and fireworks debris. He peered over the bar. "You still alive, you bastard?"

Yuri's eyes slid over to Rich. "*Da*. Nikolai?" He sounded frightened.

"Dead."

The big man turned away. He wailed softly.

"I'm going to enjoy watching you fry."

Tom's twisted body sat in puddles of blood, brain and tissue. Dark matted blood glistened in his beard.

"I owe you, Tom. I'll take care of Laurie, Jimmy and...Daisy."

The stainless steel cooler behind the bar was shot up and covered in glass and booze. Rich leaned over the bar and opened the cooler. All the ice had melted. Yellow discolored water swam about punctured beer cans and broken bottles. Rich carefully picked through and found two intact cans of Heineken. He slipped one in the bag of ammo and pulled the tab of the second. He drank.

"Open your mouth, soldier," he said to Yuri.

The big Russian opened his mouth.

Rich poured a long stream of beer, splashing Yuri's face and filling his mouth. The Russian coughed and swallowed. Rich let the empty can fall; glancing off Yuri's wet face.

"*Spasibo*," the big man said breathless, coughing again.

"Nicky said that. What's it mean?"

"It mean...thanks."

Rich turned away.

He slipped in blood as he kicked Dedmon's carcass away from the front door. "Piece of shit." Rich pulled the door open.

"I'm coming out. Don't shoot."

Stepping into the sunlight, Rich held the Springfield in his right hand, the nylon bag in his left with arms upraised.

A helicopter hovered above.

"Drop the weapon."

"Let me see your hands."

"No."

"Drop it."

"On the ground."

Nicky's orange Mercury was still out front.

"We will shoot."

"I am not going to fire. Don't shoot." Rich went down to his knees.

"On the pavement."

Advancing fast, with automatic weapons at eye level, police in green Kevlar, goggles and helmets, swarmed from the front and rear, surrounding Rich.

"Drop the weapon."

Dressed all in black with a big white FBI logo on his chest, Bertoloni broke through the circle of police. "Lower your weapons. He's the good guy."

The police looked from Rich to Bertoloni. They kept their weapons trained on Rich.

"Where the hell have you been, Bertoloni?"

"Here. Soon as the call came in from Lavender."

"Why didn't you come in?" Rich lowered his arms.

One of the police looked from Bertoloni to Rich. "He said to hold off."

"I figured that..."

Slowly the police let their weapons down and straightened from a crouch.

"I was the bait, wasn't I?" Rich struggled to his feet. "You wanted Nicky to show—then you could nail him. If he killed me in the process--who cares. That's a big promotion for you." Rich went for Bertoloni. One of the police restrained him.

"Easy, buddy."

Bertoloni replied with a smirk. "All of this could've been avoided if you'd turned over your notes and sources to us."

Rich, with jaw tense, leveled narrow eyes on the agent. "You think this wouldn't have happened if I gave you my sources?" He opened the door of the Mercury, tossing the Springfield and bag onto the back seat. "You don't know Russians. This was pure revenge."

Irina huddled on the floorboards.

"Get the hell out of there." Rich ordered.

Tears smeared her black mascara and red lipstick. Blue eye liner and rouge ran down her face. She resembled a circus clown having a nervous breakdown.

"*Nyet...nyet...*" she cried.

Rich grabbed her thin wrist. She kicked and screamed but he pulled her out, flinging her into the arms of two surprised Omaha Police. "Take her to ICE and get her back to her family in Slovenia. And get her some underwear."

A siren cut off.

"Is that the ambulance? Lieutenant Lavender is shot up pretty bad, but he's still alive." Rich sorted through Nicky's keys, moving to the trunk. "There's a big Russian behind the bar—alive, shot through both legs and shoulders. He killed my friend Tom." Rich leaned down and inserted the key in the lock. "A dirty cop named Dedmon is dead behind the door. I shot him in the chest with a shot gun." He paused, his hand on the upraised trunk. "You want to arrest me, go right ahead."

An ambulance threaded its way through spectators and barricades on Vinton Street.

A police commander came up. "What's going on? Why isn't this man in cuffs?"

"He's the victim."

"I don't give a fuck. He should be in cuffs until we sort this shit out."

Bertoloni held up his hand. "Don't touch him."

"I've got reports of two foreign nationals in a shootout. There's an Omaha Police Lieutenant in there, I don't know if he's dead or alive. How can you..."

"I said to stand down. This is an FBI case."

He seethed a moment in silence, but the commander backed away.

Bertoloni turned to Rich. "Where's Nicky?"

Two black satchels and assorted rifles and ammo littered the trunk. Rich unzipped a bag. Clear plastic packets of white powder filled the bag. The second satchel had bundles American, Canadian, Mexican and Russian currency of various denominations. Rich tucked the money bag under the spare tire. He took a box of 9mm and 30-06 ammo.

"He's upstairs."

"Dead?"

"He grabbed for the gun in my hand. The son of a bitch killed my Roommate. It was either him or me." Rich tossed the black bag of dope onto the sidewalk. "Add drug dealer to the charges against Nicky." He slammed the trunk closed. "I bet you could get the big Russian to rat on who slit Bill More's throat in Park Forest. Hell...it was probably him."

"*Jefe? Jefe?*" Jorge, still wearing his food stained apron and hair net, shouted from across the street. Police and TV crews blocked him from getting through the barricades.

"Let him come."

Jorge ran up, his face twisted in shock. "*que es pasa?*"

"Jorge," Rich held the cook by his shoulder. "Listen to me. Once they're done, lock up The Ordinary. I will be back."

"Daisy," he breathlessly said. "Daisy, she ask...is *Senor* Tom *bueno?*"

"*Senor* Tom is dead."

Jorge's chin fell to his chest. His thumb and fingers made a small sign of the cross.

"And patch the windows upstairs and downstairs. Jorge, upstairs is Roommate. Would you put him in a box? I'll bury him."

"Ayyyyy, Roomy. *Si...si...Jefe.*"

"Where do you think you're going? You need to see a doctor, you're wounded."

Rich pushed past Bertoloni, opening the driver's door. "Suka thinks I'm dead. If she finds out Nicky's dead she's going after my wife."

"You can't just go and kill her."

"I'm not. Once she finds out about Nicky she'll flip. I'm going to protect my wife."

EMTs in blue uniforms with yellow vests hustled into The Ordinary with a stretcher. Gray smoke drifted out the door.

"Let us take care of it," Bertoloni said.

Police followed the EMTs into The Ordinary, while others drifted back to the barricades.

"Like you took care of this?" Rich turned and put Nicky's and his own cell phone on the seat, with the ammo and sat behind the steering wheel. He slammed the door. Reaching, he moved the seat back. Rich turned the key in the ignition and the Mercury roared to life. He pulled the gear shift on the column down to D.

"I don't condone any of this," Bertoloni shouted as Rich pulled away. "I can have you arrested."

In the rear view mirror Rich saw Bertoloni on his phone.

Nicky's phone lit up. A text box in Russian came on screen. Lines of Russian that Rich couldn't read, the signature Suka had smiley emoticons following it.

"She fell for it," Rich murmured easing through barricades, spectators and police cars, up 16th street to the interstate. "I hope I can get to Gisele in time."

Chapter 12

The big car hurtled east on Interstate 80. Rich pushed the speed limit, testing the 7 to 10 miles per hour margin. The Mercury drove like a barge, wide and heavy. But it could move. Rich wrestled the large steering wheel maneuvering in and out of traffic. He held the cold Heineken can to the back of his neck, fighting a throbbing headache.

The interior of the Mercury shined with polished walnut, chrome accents and white plastic. CDs were strewn about the leather upholstered bench type front seat. Rich glanced away from the road, sorting through discs by Gene Vincent, Stray Cats, Bill Haley, Eddie Cochran, Leningrad and Sektor Gaza. Nothing he cared to hear.

He sped by Semis, sedans, SUVs, pickup trucks and vans over the Missouri River bridge into Iowa. Congested traffic through Council Bluffs slowed Rich and tried his patience. But with the river town in the rear view mirror, Rich accelerated.

He texted Gisele: Call me.

From the Dubuque trip, Rich knew it took about five maybe six hours to drive across Iowa. That's following the posted speed limit. When he hit Illinois he had another four hours to get to Glencoe on the North Shore. He didn't know if he could hold off Suka for nine hours. She couldn't be fooled that long. TV or print news would pick up the story. Eventually Suka would find out her son Nicky had been shot and killed.

Cresting a hill at 85 mph Rich saw the gray car parked in the grassy median.

"Shit."

In the mirror he saw red and blue lights flashing on the roof, as the Iowa State Trooper pulled from the between the lanes, onto the freeway. The siren pulsed.

"I don't have time for this." For a fleeting moment he thought he might try to outrun the trooper. But he knew he couldn't. He tossed the beer can aside.

Holding at 85 mph Rich waited for the interceptor to close on his bumper. Cars in the right lane pulled over when Rich flipped on the turn signal and coasted onto the shoulder.

"Damn it," he muttered as the trooper braked behind him. Opening the glove box, a glass syringe and bag of brown dope fell to the floorboard. Rich pushed the works and baggie under the seat and sorted through papers for a pink registration. He didn't find it.

The gray uniformed trooper stepped out and adjusted his Smoky the Bear hat at a slight forward tilt. He wore aviator-style sunglasses with green-tinted lenses. The walk-up seemed an exaggerated and slow swagger. Knuckles rapped on the window.

"There a problem officer?" Rich rolled down the window.

"Do you know how fast you were driving?"

"Yeah...about 85," Rich replied in a matter of fact tone. "If I thought I could've got away with it I would've been doing 100."

"Step out of the car, please." The trooper moved away from the door.

"Listen, officer. This is a matter of life and death." Rich grimaced, bumping his wounded arm on the door as he climbed out. The trooper noticed. "I have to get to Glencoe, Illinois as soon as possible. My wife lives there and she's in danger." In the periphery of his sight, Rich saw the Springfield laying across the backseat. He sidestepped and stood, blocking the passenger window.

"Can I see your license?"

A second gray interceptor pulled up behind the first car and an Iowa State trooper stepped out.

Rich's heart sank. He reached to his back pocket for his wallet. A slight breeze opened Rich's flannel shirt. The butt of Rich's Glock in the shoulder holster showed.

The trooper's hand went to his service revolver on his hip.

"Easy, I'm just going for my wallet."

The second trooper froze.

The trooper's head twisted quickly over his shoulder. "Steve...do me a favor, get your first aid kit."

"I'm telling you the truth." Rich pulled his license from the plastic sleeve in his wallet. "I've got to get to Glencoe. My wife's in danger."

The trooper took the white license. He held it up and checked Rich in the photo. "Richard Rice."

"Yes." Rich sighed. "Just write me a ticket and let me go."

The second trooper came up with a white first aid kit.

"I'm sorry I had to put you through that, Mr. Rice."
The trooper handed Rich his license back. "I had to make
sure it was you."

"What do you mean?"

"We got a call about you." The thinnest of thin smiles
sneaked across the trooper's face.

The second trooper opened the kit and put on blue
rubber gloves. He went around to Rich's bloody arm. "Let
me take a look at that," he said.

"Who called you?"

"FBI notified us to be on the lookout for you and assist
in your travels across Iowa. My commander is as giddy as a
schoolgirl at the Barbie doll store. Seldom does the FBI ask
him for favors."

The second trooper carefully tore open the burned and
bloody sleeve, exposing the wounded bicep. "Not too bad.
But it needs to be dressed." He picked through the first aid
kit and took out disinfectant, gauze pad, tape and a roll of
gauze. "Can you take off your shirt?" Gingerly, Rich eased
his arm out. The trooper studied Rich's Glock. "Nice side
arm there. And excuse me for saying, but you look like shit.
Is that dried blood on your face? You've gray dust and bits
of glass and paper in your hair." He reached into the kit
and took out a wet nap packet. "Here, clean yourself up."

Walking around, inspecting the Mercury, the trooper
exclaimed: "Woo, baby. This is some bucket of bolts." He
paused. "Is this your car?"

"No," Rich answered. The lemon scented wet nap was
cool and refreshing on his face. "It's a loaner."

"Think she can do a hundred twenty?"

"I don't..." Rich winced as the trooper sprayed
disinfectant on his wound. "...don't know."

"Mind if I pop the hood?"

"Go right ahead."

He reached down and pulled the hood latch. "Holy crap. This is a 408w full roller super charged mill with aluminum heads. This baby can deliver about 440 horsepower. Why'd you stop? If you'd floored it I would've had a helluva time trying to catch you." The trooper peered around the upraised hood. "Five or six-speed shifter?"

"Automatic."

"Automatic?" The trooper slammed down the hood. "Now that is a damn shame."

The second trooper taped a pad over Rich's wound, then wrapped gauze around his bicep. "That should hold you. But listen," the trooper gave Rich a stern look. "It looks like some glass or metal fragments are still in there. You need to see a doctor as soon as you can."

"Will do. Thanks, Officer."

"Okay, Mr. Rice." The trooper came up and folded his arms. "Like I said, we've been requested to escort you in your journey through the great state of Iowa. How much gas you got?"

"Last I looked, about three-quarters of a tank."

"Good." The trooper started for his interceptor. "He all patched up, Steve?"

"He'll live." Snapping closed the first aid kit and tearing off the rubber gloves, the trooper started back to his interceptor.

"With the engine you got in that sled maybe we should put the circus lights on your roof. But here's the plan." The trooper opened the door to his interceptor. "Stay close. Flash your lights if you have a problem."

Rich slipped on his shirt and opened the driver's door.

"C'mon," the trooper grinned. "Let's light'em up, scare the population and all small animals."

KEEPER OF AN ORDINARY | 221

Blue lights flashing, siren wailing, the trooper pulled out. Rich gunned the engine and stepped on the accelerator. The big Mercury, spewing rocks and gravel, hit the blacktop and laid a loud and long patch of blue smoking burned rubber. He tucked in behind the trooper and matched his speed. The needle climbed to 100 mph and held steady for long stretches of the interstate. The citizenry did indeed scatter before them. They swerved right, cars and Semis slowed, letting the interceptor and vintage Mercury rip by. Passing cars looked like they were standing still.

Coming into Des Moines the two vehicles let up, averaging 80 miles an hour. On the other side of town, they put the pedal down. Rich realized he'd cut the usual two hour travel time to less than an hour. If they could maintain this pace he'd cross Iowa in two hours plus. Iowa City forced another slackening of the speed. A second gray Iowa state interceptor drove alongside. The trooper pointed to Rich, then to himself. He sped up and slipped between and the first interceptor. The first car pulled aside, drawing level with Rich. He gave the trooper a salute. The trooper appeared to laugh, waved, then peeled off heading for an upcoming exit.

Nicky's phone buzzed. Rich gripped the steering wheel tightly and didn't dare answer. He let it go to voice mail. He took his own phone and texted Gisele again: Call me.

Interstate 80 beyond Iowa City had bad patches of road bed. Rich concentrated on the road ahead for cracks and pot holes. The old Mercury, built as solid as a battleship, still thumped and shook with every hole. They roared past the sprawling Iowa 80 rest stop.

The round, old style white dial gas gauge dipped under a quarter of a tank. Rich flashed his headlights. The trooper eased off and gave way to Rich to pull ahead. They approached Davenport. Rich exited, turning into the first gas station. The trooper got out and walked up to Rich as he came out of the convenience store and crossed to the gas pumps. Opening a bottle of water, he drank long before jerking the gas nozzle from its holder.

"Woo, now that was some fun." Young, with a military style crew cut, the trooper flashed a row of white teeth.

"Thanks for getting me across Iowa, quickly."

"So are you a rock star, or a politician?"

"No, nothing like that." Rich scrolled down his contacts and highlighted Gisele's number.

"Our 'net traffic is on fire with guys volunteering to 'open'er up'. You're the one they're talking about." The trooper noticed the bandage through the tears in Rich's sleeve. Blood spotted the white gauze. "You all right?"

His phone on his ear, Rich glanced at his arm. "Fine."

"Maybe you should see a doctor."

"No time. I have to get to Glencoe ASAP." Gisele's phone went to voice mail. "Damn."

"I can escort you through Davenport, but once you're on the bridge, I got to let you go."

Rich replaced the gas nozzle and screwed on the gas cap. "Thanks again."

"Ready to roll?"

Rich stayed with the trooper and waved as the interceptor took the last exit before the Mississippi River Bridge.

The Iowa State troopers escort had cut Rich's cross-state, border-to-border time from almost five hours to just over two hours. Almost surreal, Rich realized just a couple hours ago he had emerged, with hands up, from the smoke, debris and death of the shot up Ordinary. He had to get to

Gisele. "Halfway," Rich thought as he crossed the bridge to East Moline. Maintaining 75 miles an hour seemed a crawl as he climbed up the bluffs on the Illinois side.

The flashing blue and red light bar filled his rear view mirror. Sliding alongside, an Illinois State Trooper made a pumping motion with his fist. Rich let the trooper speed out front; then matched the trooper's 90-95 mph.

"Okay, Bertoloni," Rich muttered. "Maybe I owe you for this."

Now in Illinois Rich again phoned Gisele. If he kept this pace, he had two maybe three hours before reaching Glencoe. If Suka, or her gang, were listening in to Gisele's phone they'd find Rich alive. He'd take that chance. No answer. He cracked open the beer and took a drink.

Weariness came over him. The concentration it took to trail the troopers at a high rate of speed almost drained him. The intensity of the gun fight at The Ordinary, the moments of sheer terror, had taken a toll on his body and mind. The wound on his arm ached. He stretched out the arm to keep it from stiffening. He would not let up. He couldn't. Gisele's life depended on him. He dialed 411.

A woman's tired voice answered. "Directory assistance, what city and state?"

"Glencoe, Illinois. I need the number of the Glencoe Police Department."

"Hold please."

"Come on."

Near Aurora and the junction of 294 North, the trooper waved and left the road ahead open to Rich. He had 40 miles left to get to Glencoe.

Nicky's phone buzzed again. The text consisted of lines of Russian, ending with a series of question marks. The text worried Rich.

"I'm sorry, sir," the directory assistance woman said. "I can't find a listing for Glencoe Police."

"What? That's crazy. They have to have a police department."

"Sir. There is a listing for the Glencoe Public Safety Department."

"That's it. Please connect me."

"It's not the police, sir."

"No, it is, it is. I know it."

Through the western suburbs and driving north, the last time he took this route Dedmon drove as Rich nursed his wounded side. Much had transpired since.

"Dispatch Glencoe Public Safety."

The words just rushed out. "My name is Richard Rice. My wife, Gisele Esslin lives on Sheridan Street. She may be in extreme danger."

"Mr. Rice? Are you known as Keeper?"

"Yes, yes, that's me."

"We got a call from Omaha FBI about you. There are patrol cars enroute to the Esslin house."

"That's good." The relief came through Rich's voice. "I'm on my way."

"No," the dispatch operator's voice rose. "Mr. Rice, don't...."

"Thanks." Rich clicked off while the operator kept talking.

Autumn leaves of the woodsy North Shore community glowed red, yellow and orange. Wind off Lake Michigan sent clouds of leaves crossing the road, piling up like snow drifts.

Turning onto Green Bay Road Rich called Gisele. It rang once, then twice. In the middle of the third ring someone picked up.

'Who this?" The voice was a husky, woman's voice.

"Gisele?" Rich didn't recognize the voice.

He hung up.

Dusk approached, the sky turned a steely gray.

White and green patrol cars from Glencoe Public Safety and blue Winnetka Police patrol cars, red lights spinning lined either side of the street. Officers in black bullet proof vests, helmets and armed with assault rifles leaned on the cars staring down the street.

A pair of officers stepped into the street, hands up stopping Rich. He rolled down the window. "What's going on?"

"Sheridan Street is closed, sir." A young bushy haired officer in a green uniform bent to the window. The second officer followed, slouching with the heel of his hand resting on his gun butt.

"No, you don't understand. I have to get to my house."

"There's a hostage situation in progress. No one is allowed access onto Sheridan Street."

"Hostage?" Rich floored the accelerator pedal.

The officers leapt back. Both guns came out. Other officers put their hands up in front of Rich. But they couldn't stop him as he swerved onto Sheridan, a tree-canopied street fronting three story estates and palatial red brick homes set well back from the road. He slowed. The street seemed to doze peacefully as bushes shivered in a breeze between hedges yet green, lush and tall enough for a man to get lost among. A half block from Gisele's mother's house Rich spotted a black Mercedes parked across the street.

Rich stopped just down from Gisele's drive. Wind scattered fallen leaves. He stared at the Mercedes and shadowy figures sitting inside. Then both doors opened.

From the passenger side a small, old looking big boned woman with short pumpkin orange hair stepped out. She wore a long drab gray skirt, light brown jumper that resembled burlap and two-tone white and brown cowboy boots. A tall man in a black suit stepped from the driver's side. Without a doubt, the woman was Suka. She ran on short stumpy legs toward the Mercury.

"Nikolai."

Rich watched her come.

"Nikolai."

Taking the Glock from his holster, snapping back the receiver and chambering a round, Rich opened the heavy door and stood.

Suka froze in her tracks. A stunned look contorted her round face. "Is you. You. Where my Nikolai?"

The tall man jogged up to Suka's side. He held a MAC11 at his waist.

"It's over, Suka."

"Where my Nicky?" Suka's complexion reddened, her voice rising.

"I said it's over."

"Not over." Suka yelled. "Where my *malysh?*"

The car door shielded Rich. He studied the tall man while Suka swung her arms and stamped her boots.

"You tell," she bellowed. "Police? Police take my Nicky?" Panting hard, her eyes blazing, Suka shook.

"No."

Time stood still a moment.

"Where? You tell."

"He's in the bone yard."

Suka threw back her head and from the depths of her womb let out a piercing scream—a mother's keening. She grabbed for the MAC11, tearing it from the tall man's grasp.

"You kill my Nikolai." Her head swaying side to side, the brick and stick style machine pistol jumped in Suka's hands as she sprayed bullets in the trees and down the street. The tall man reached inside his suit coat.

Rich stepped away from the car, crouched and put two quick shots in the center of the tall man's chest. He went down with his hand still inside his coat.

Suka seemed to gather herself seeing the tall man tumble behind her. Her eyes like cold black lasers, she shot at Rich and the Mercury, exploding a headlight, shattering the windshield, sewing a line of bullet holes from the fender to the driver's door.

Ducking behind the trunk, Rich reached over the fender and snapped off a couple of rounds at Suka.

She stooped and snatched magazines from the coat pocket of the tall man then ran toward the Mercedes.

Expecting the Russian to make an escape Rich came around from the back of the Mercury.

An elderly couple walked up their driveway, looking about curiously. "What's all the noise out here?" the man asked Rich.

"Get back in your house. It's not safe out here."

The older woman had a cell phone in her hand. "Should I call the police?"

At the Mercedes Suka spun on her boot heel and leveled the MAC11.

"Get down," Rich called, diving behind a parked car as bullets zipped through the trees and bushes.

The old woman gasped as the man stepped in front and pushed her back.

Rich scrambled to his feet. Sirens sounded in the distance.

"Oh, no you don't." He sprinted around the Mercury. Glass particles littered the car's interior. He brushed off the seat and got in. The engine coughed as it cranked. Smoke and colored liquid spewed out the front grill, but the engine turned over. Rich dropped the gear shift to D and stomped the accelerator. The Mercury bucked and balked, but moved forward.

A Glencoe Public Safety patrol car came up behind Rich. A second patrol car skidded to a stop sideways in the middle of the street, in front of the tall man's sprawled body.

Rich braked near the entrance to Gisele's circular drive.

Four green uniformed Glencoe cops jumped out of the cars, guns drawn.

"Get out of the car."

"Reach for the sky."

Rich stepped out, hands raised. "I'm not the one you want." Sighing, second time today cops pointing guns at me, he thought.

Two cops, one black, the other white, scooted to the Mercury, leading with their guns.

"Did you say *Reach for the sky*?" The black cop gave the other cop a bewildered look.

Cringing, the white cop said: "I did." His eyes rolled upward.

"Way to go, lil buckeroo. The crazy white people I have to work with." The black cop lowered his side arm. "Are you Rice?"

"The Keeper guy?"

"That's me."

"Put your hands down. Some dude from the FBI called, telling the chief you were headed this way. We got here and took some shots from the black Mercedes. We set up a perimeter—which you busted through. There's a hostage in the Mercedes.

"Who's the guy in the street?"

"Bratva, Russian Mafia."

Shouting could be heard from inside the Mercedes.

"She's got my wife."

One cop grabbed Rich's shirt tail jerking him down behind the Mercury's fender. "What the hell you think you're gonna do?"

"We got Winnetka PD here."

"FBI also."

"That's reassuring."

"Who's in there?"

"A Russian woman named Suka. I'm the one she wants," Rich said.

The sedan door banged open and Gisele emerged with her hands zip-tied behind her. At her back, the shorter Suka had Gisele's shirt collar bunched in her fist. Suka had the MAC11 pointed at Gisele's head.

Rich and the two cops held their guns over the Mercury hood trained on Suka.

"Stay back. I keel des beech. Stay back." Suka kept Gisele as a shield.

Gisele's face glowed red, her eyes big and scared.

"Drop Gisele," Rich shouted.

"I can't," she replied in a quivering voice.

"You got nowhere to go lady."

Over screaming sirens Suka yelled back. "That what you think."

"If you harm my wife..." Rich stood.

"You keel my Nicky." Suka squeezed of a short burst.

The black cop tackled Rich. "Son of a bitch. Will you keep your head down?"

"We got SWAT, snipers, negotiators...we'll get her to give up."

Suka dragged Rich's wife into the Mercedes.

"She's going to run." Rich holstered his Glock and went to the back seat, pulling out the scoped Springfield. He opened the bolt and pushed in a five-round stripper, then locked it.

A narrow-shouldered, big bottomed Winnetka Police officer in blue uniform festooned with medals, ribbons and a gold badge, scuttled up. "What we got, boys?" He seemed breathless and excited.

"Where's your weapon, sir?"

Police cars, with flashing lights, edged forward, blocking Sheridan Street at the far corner.

Rich gave the officer a sidelong glance. "Who the hell are you?"

"Captain Hager," the officer replied. "Don't do anything stupid, fellows. We got property and people...and property to protect."

Rich raised the rifle and watched Suka through the reticle.

"You want this beech to leef, you stay back," she yelled out the car window.

They could hear Gisele screaming and swearing.

Putting a hand on the black cop's shoulder, Rich asked: "What's your name?"

"Ah...it's Terry." He didn't appear to understand the reason for the question.

"Terry, if that was your wife...?" Rich, with steady eyes on the cop, let the question hang.

"What're you guys thinking?" the Captain asked.

Suka started the Mercedes. She riddled the street with the MAC11. The black sedan made a violent U-turn.

"You drive," Rich said to Terry.

"Don't do it, Terry."

Terry pressed his lips together tightly. He glanced down and exhaled loudly.

Suka gunned the engine.

"What you said about it being my wife." Terry paused. "Let's go."

They dashed to the patrol car, with Rich hopping into the passenger seat. Terry settled behind the wheel and started the engine.

Rich rolled down the window pointing the rifle barrel out. "Get on her ass."

"Hang on." The patrol car squealed out, in pursuit of the Mercedes. "Where she going?"

Suka swerved to the right, and sped up halfway through the turn.

"Why?"

"The highway is to the left. Does she think she can drive across Lake Michigan?"

Terry floored the patrol car until it was right on Suka's back bumper. Through the rear window Rich saw the two women fighting as she drove. He took aim.

"You shoot from a moving vehicle," Terry shouted over the rushing wind and engine noise. "You might hit your wife."

"Shit." Rich lowered the rifle. "I could shoot out the tires."

Police cars barricaded the street ahead. Two cops were laying out star strips.

"She's screwed now."

"I just need a clear shot."

"Keep it low."

Suka veered left onto Park Street.

"Now what's she thinking?" Terry crossed hand over hand on the steering wheel.

"Where's this go?"

"The parking lot at Lake Front Park. I don't get it—she's trapped."

The Mercedes sped to the end of the street and crashed through a saw horse with a Closed for the Season sign at the parking lot entrance.

"Keep back."

Terry swung the patrol car just inside the lot, blocking the exit.

Suka struggled out of the Mercedes dragging Gisele after. She kicked at Suka. The Russian woman backhanded Gisele hard across the face with the MAC11. The blow staggered her. With a firm grip on Gisele, Suka pulled the stunned woman toward the beach.

"Come on." Rich, with Terry following, jogged across the lot.

Patrol cars, with sirens screaming and lights spinning pulled up behind Terry's patrol car.

Suka, her hostage in tow, ran down a black asphalt path to the beach. Stone walls bordered the pathway.

Rich smelled dead fish and a faint sulfur stink of the lake, they were that close. He rounded the top and Suka took a couple of shots at him. He dodged behind a lamp post. Bullets snapped by his head and ricocheted off the wall.

At the bottom of the path Suka jerked Gisele through an arched stone building and onto the beach.

Terry trailed as Rich ran through the building. A stiff chilling breeze blew off the lake.

"I don't know what this crazy bitch is thinking." Terry said, breathing hard. "She thinks she can swim for it?"

Suka struggled running through sand, pulling Rich's wife. A single low watt street light glowed orange at the top of a long pole above the pavilion. Rhythmic waves splashed onto the beach.

The gray sky and gray lake, with oncoming night, disguised where lake and sky met as if spilling over into the invisible, the purple gray horizon. A long wrought iron fence painted white bordered a concrete pier extending out into the lake from a pavilion on the beach. A red navigation light blinked on and off atop the long pole at the end. Pushing Gisele, the two reached the pier.

Rich squatted behind a square stone garbage can.

A go-fast boat cut across the water, its running lights on. The sleek hulled boat came out of the bright orange glow from the Lake Shore cities to the south.

"You think that boat's for her?" Terry pointed.

"I'd bet on it."

Suka dragged Gisele to the end of the pier. "Stay back or I shoot da beech."

"If the boat stops, I'll put a couple of rounds in the engine compartment and see if I can disable it."

"If she gets on that boat," Terry said to Rich. "She can go a long ways north...as far as Canada."

Rich set up behind pilings, sighting in on Suka.

Gisele had collapsed at Suka's feet.

Police lights filled the parking lot above the beach.

A strong wet wind stung Rich's forehead and cheek. He moved the reticle to the boat. The long craft bounced in the mil-dot sight. Three men, one at the helm, stood in the boat. Pain shot up Rich's arm as he slipped his left arm over the butt of the rifle, placing his left hand on his right shoulder.

"It's about 80 yards." Terry knelt next to Rich. "A steady breeze...right to left."

The go-fast boat throttled back, angling for the pier.

"It's coming into the pier."

Crack. The shot echoed off the water and concrete walls of the park buildings. Rich put a round in the stern just above the water line. Startled and noisy about it, dirty white seagulls took to wing. He jerked the bolt up and back. A shiny brass casing jumped out the breech, tumbling to the pavement. He pushed the bolt forward and down. *Crack.* Smoke billowed out the back of the speed boat. *Crack.* The man behind the wheel pitched over the side. Seagulls swirled in the gray sky above the pavilion.

Suka shot down the pier. Terry grunted, grabbing his left thigh. Bullets thumped into the wood pilings.

The go-fast boat, trailing smoke, bumped into the end of the pier.

"I keel da beech."

Through the scope in the gathering dark, Rich put the dotted cross on Suka. The wind went still. Suka held the MAC11 to Gisele's head. Rich let out a breath. He set the mil-dot just high right and above Suka's round orange head. "Relax," he heard his dad whisper. Rich squeezed the trigger.

Crack.

Suka fell back against the railing, her arms dropping to her sides. The MAC11 clattered to the concrete of the pier.

Gisele crawled away.

"You all right, Terry?"

"Yeah. I got tagged in the thigh. Go get your wife."

"Give me your knife."

Police cars eased down the path to the beach.

With the Springfield aimed from his hip, Rich ran to Gisele.

Two men from the boat grabbed Suka and pulled her over the railing. Someone shot. The go-fast boat pushed off from the pier, and backed away.

Crying, she fell into Rich's arms. "I thought she was going to kill me. I thought I was dead."

In the half-light Rich saw Gisele's face. Her eye, as red as an onion, had swollen. Bloody scratches scored the side of her face. Under her eye a deep gash followed the arch of her cheek bone. He took the tail of his shirt and dabbed at the blood on her chin and cheek.

"Did I kill her?" Rich cut the plastic zip-tie off her wrists.

"I don't know." Gisele wiped tears from her eyes, grimacing. "The noise of the boat, the waves breaking against the pier, they were yelling in Russian, but I heard a hollow pop, then that bitch sighed and her grip on my collar relaxed. I looked back and she seemed to be leaning against the railing, her eyes open. Soon as I could I got away." She rubbed her wrists.

Cops, with weapons drawn, hustled by them as they walked to the beach.

The engine of the go-fast boat roared. Still smoking the craft cut a long wake, heading north.

EMTs put Terry on a wheeled stretcher.

"You okay?" Rich asked, handing back the knife.

"Been better."

"Thanks." Rich patted him on the shoulder.

"Any time. You all right, Missus?"

Gisele nodded.

"Take care." The EMTs rolled Terry off the pier and carried him across the beach.

"She kept saying you killed her son. What happened today?"

"Nicky showed up at The Ordinary. We shot it out."

"Tom?"

Rich shook his head side-to-side.

"Oh my god, Rich. Daisy?"

"She and Jorge are okay."

"Roomy?"

His head dropped.

"Nope." Rich stopped. "What's this shit?"

Captain Hager and a short, pear-shaped, balding man in a dark blue suit came toward them. "Mr. Rice?"

"Am I in trouble?"

"I don't think so," the man assured him. He had a triangle of short curly hair about the size of a merkin on the crown of his head. "But we have a helluva lot of crap to sort out. Can you come with us?"

"My wife needs medical attention."

"Actually, I need a cigarette. Anybody got a cigarette?"

Hager motioned to a patrolman. "Take Mrs. Rice to an ambulance. And get her statement."

The balding man brushed forward his fuzzy patch. "I wonder if this mess could've been avoided had you supplied the bureau with your information."

"Who told you that?"

"Agent Bertoloni has kept me quite well informed."

Rich motioned to the north. "You're letting them get away."

"Not your concern, Mr. Rice," the bald man said. A low flying black helicopter skimmed the waves, followed by two swift boats. The craft, marked FBI, ran with lights out and followed Suka's go-fast boat north. "We're interested to see where they put in." The man rocked on his heels, wearing a pursed lipped smile. "Shall we go?"

The patrolman came up.

"Wait a second. Gisele..." Rich pulled out Nicky's keys from his pocket. He turned Gisele away and speaking low, said: "The orange Mercury sitting at the end of your driveway...the same car from Dubuque...it's ours now. Drive it into your garage. In the trunk, under the spare tire, there's a black satchel. Take it. Hide it."

"What is it?"

"The spoils of war."

"Rich, is this bullshit finally over?"

He looked toward the north, over the murky gray lake. Barely visible in the distance were running lights and a trail of smoke.

"For now, maybe, Gisele."

Chapter 13

It was a municipal gray interrogation room, the grayest of gray rooms in the basement of the mock colonial suburban Winnetka Police station. With its long slate hued table, pewter chairs and rat-colored walls and linoleum, the room appeared grayer than all indifference. Overcome by a bone weariness Rich lay his forehead on a folded arm. Across the room a tinted glass window hid others watching him. The room seemed neither too warm nor too cold. Dinginess might've lent character to the drab surroundings, something more interesting than the vague odor of *Lysol*.

Opposite Rich sat three men: the balding chunky blue suited man from the pier at Lake Front Park, a nondescript middle aged man of medium build wearing a dappled gray flannel suit, and Bertoloni dressed in faded black combat fatigues and seated at the corner of the table. The young agent's face looked drawn, his complexion sallow, with dark, drooping eyes. It'd been a full day for him as well.

Rich noticed a plastic dome fixed in the middle of the ceiling of sound dampening perforated tile. A red light glowed faintly inside the dome. He wondered how many middle fingers, fuck yous and insincere smiles had been recorded by that camera.

"Tell us again how the fight started."

Rich raised his head. His eyes were hot. He rubbed them. "I've told you already, three times."

"We've just got the preliminary crime scene reports and want to make sure we have the sequence correct." The bald man's round head leaned back on his fat neck as he looked at Rich through half-lidded eyes.

His name was FBI Agent Jejune or something Rich's dead tired brain couldn't absorb when introduced. Not that he cared. Three pairs of eyes, brown, brown and blue and who knew how many eyes observed behind the tinted window.

"Nicky and three others came into The Ordinary." Rich slumped in his chair trying to rouse his energy with a deep breath. He moved his arm. The wound ached and his muscles had gone stiff and sore.

"How did Mr. Franko find out where you were?" Jejune had a posh breathy voice. Every word sounded blown off his palate and through his lips.

Rich opened his eyes, focusing on the agent. The florescent light hurt. "They tricked my wife. They followed her to a post office and two of Nicky's whores got their hands on a letter Gisele was sending to me. They got the address off the letter."

The three agents scribbled on white legal pads.

"They showed up at your bar in Omaha?" Jejune toyed with the triangle bush atop his fleshy pate.

"Two days later."

"Yes, it was Nikolai Franko and...?"

"Some underage girl. A big guy named Yuri..."

"Yuri Grimansky," the middle agent interrupted. "He was ex-Soviet military with tours in Afghanistan and Chechnya. The girl was Irina Pushkin, aged 13; reported missing by her family in Slovenia."

"Yeah...and Dedmon."

"The rouge Chicago cop, part of the human trafficking task force, but working both ends of the deal."

"Tom Waller..."

Bertoloni cut Rich off. "Okay, we got the scene. Who shot first?"

Rich sighed, eyes to the ceiling. "Lt. Lavender pulled out his revolver and shouted for Nicky and the others to put their hands on the bar. All three went for their weapons. Yuri had an AK-74 and just blasted the hell out of Lavender. I got a chance to flip Tom my .38..."

"Mr. Waller was unarmed?"

"Yes." Rich waited for any follow up. "I told him to take out Yuri. I pulled out a shotgun from under the bar."

"So Lt. Lavender was shot first?" Jejune pushed out and puckered his lips while thoughtfully tapping a pen on his temple. His top lip wrinkled deeply like the frown of a mean old woman.

"Yes. Then I shot Dedmon at the door...and Tom put a couple of rounds in Yuri's shoulder."

"That's when Grimansky turned the Kalashnikov on Mr. Waller..." Jejune wrote. "So...let me see if I have the sequence correct. Yuri and Nicky shot Lt. Lavender. You shot and killed Dedmon." He counted out the lives on his short fingers. "Yuri shot and killed Mr. Waller..."

Jejune's hands were soft, fleshy, pink and clean. His manicured nails were evenly clipped and shiny. Rich gazed at his rough hands. The nails were chipped and hoarded lines of dirt underneath. Dark blue bruises and blood blisters speckled the cuticles. Short bloody cuts crisscrossed the ground-in dirt on Rich's calloused palms. The crook of his right hand showed vague bluish discoloration, from absorbing the weapons recoil. Two grooves of red irritation, with flaked skin, ran from the web of his hand to the base of his thumb--receiver cuts. Long, narrow and strong, if he needed he could ball up his hand into a fist of hard bone and big knuckles.

They were in suits while Rich wore a dirty t-shirt and flannel over shirt with a ripped left sleeve stained brownish and stiff from dried blood—his blood and Gisele's blood.

"No...Tom shot Yuri in the shoulder."

"Oh yes, yes...then Yuri shot Mr. Waller. And later Yuri tried to jump the bar where you were hiding. You shot and wounded him." He checked his pad. "Who did Nikolai Franko shoot?"

An interval of silence separated each side of the table. The florescent lights hummed.

"Nicky Franko admitted he was the sniper that took a shot at me. He was about to shoot me when he killed my Roommate."

"Your roommate?"

"That's the dog." The middle agent chimed in. "That doesn't count."

"What do you mean it doesn't count?"

"Did you get shot in the arm?"

"No..." Rich glanced at his left arm. "A large piece of flying glass got me."

"How come you didn't get shot?"

"Nicky was a lousy shot."

"You have bruises on your chin, neck and, you told us, your shoulders. How did you get those?"

"Nicky kicked me in the face. Before that he hit me with a chair. He was about to shoot me. Then my dog distracted him and I grabbed a knife and stabbed him."

"Wait. You stabbed him? I thought he was shot?"

"He was. I put the knife through his knee."

"And then you shot him?"

"No I didn't shoot him. I had his .357 aimed at him. He grabbed for the gun and it went off."

"He was shot though? And killed?"

"Yes."

"Witnesses?"

"None."

Three heads suddenly bowed together, speaking in heated undertones. Rich overheard: "This could be a problem in court."

The heads broke apart.

"Okay. Let's go over the Glencoe situation." Jejune twiddled his pen impatiently. "You arrived in Nikolai Franko's vehicle." He stopped, as if remembering. "Incidentally, where is that vehicle? It was not on the street when we swept the crime scene."

"I told my wife to move it off the street...into her garage...for safekeeping."

"I'll send some agents out there to get it," Mr. Middle Agent whispered.

Agent Jejune leveled a flinty stare at Bertoloni as if to say: Why'd you let Rice take the suspect's car?"

Bertoloni read the look and responded. "It played into our agreed upon strategy to let Mr. Rice act upon the situation. It brought Suka out of hiding and..."

"Okay." Jejune turned away from Bertoloni, his hand with two fingers up. "You confront Suka Franko and..." He glanced at his pad. "Dimitri Fyodor Karpov..."

"Who's that?"

"The man with Suka."

"The tall guy?"

"Yes. And Suka learns you killed her son Nikolai. She starts shooting at you."

"Yes." Rich dry washed his face, fighting exhaustion. "I mean no. I told her Nicky was dead. She assumed I killed him."

"Then you shot Karpov?"

"He went for a weapon in his coat."

"You didn't see the weapon?"

"No...he didn't mention it."

"He did indeed have a weapon in his coat. So you shot him." A third fat finger uncurled from Jejune's rosy fist. "Suka abducted your wife, taking her as a shield to Lake Front Park, where she is met by a speed boat to affect her escape."

"She assaulted my wife. And...and, she shot Terry, the Glencoe cop."

"Yes. Then you shot Suka, possibly fatally..." A fourth finger straightened.

"I shot at the boat and the guy at the wheel."

Agent Jejune's thumb popped out.

Rich started to get it. "What's going on here?"

"Mr. Rice," Jejune said. "I'm counting three confirmed fatalities, a victim with severe gunshot wounds and possibly a fourth and fifth fatal shooting--all by your hand. I don't know how we can justify these actions without putting it before a Federal grand jury."

"What? It was self-defense. They came into my business intent on killing me. I was protecting my wife."

"That may be...but I'll let a grand jury decide that."

"Why don't you just deport me to Russia."

"No need to be flippant. If you were a member of the bureau we would do a shooting review and you would probably be cleared of any wrongdoing. But you're not. We are going to have to turn it over to a grand jury."

"What the hell are you talking about?"

"He worked in a capacity that aided the bureau," Bertoloni injected. But Jejune would have none of it.

"I'm sure of that. But I am not going to have an international incident. I already am getting inquiries from the FSB, Russian Security Service and our own state department. I won't be drawn and quartered in the press and accused of a cover up because he's allowed to walk no questions asked." Jejune stood, sorting his pad and papers and tucking them tightly under his elbow.

"Are you going to arrest me?"

Jejune looked to the ceiling.

"No, we're going to release you on your own recognizance, pending an investigation and the findings of a grand jury. You may be subpoenaed to testify at the grand jury. I suggest you get a lawyer. At this point in time you are just the subject of the investigation. Your status could change. Oh, and perhaps it goes without saying, but, don't leave the country."

The middle agent followed, on Jejune's backside like bumper to bumper traffic.

The balding agent stopped at the door, turning. "And agent Bertoloni, if you want a career out in the shoot'em up Wild West that's fine. If, however, you want to move up in the bureau I would advise you to adhere to protocol. The end does not justify the means. There'll be no fake reporters, nor fast and furious problems from this office. Not on my watch."

"What the fuck, Bertoloni?" Rich said, as the door closed. "I thought we were on the same side. You set me up. And that fucker wants to fry me."

"Hold on. Hold on. I'm sure you'll be okay with the grand jury investigation. Like he said, you're a subject, not the target. Agent Jejune is just a by-the-book kind of guy."

"Then I can go?"

"Yeah, I'll escort you out."

"First escort me to a doctor so I can get my arm looked at."

Layers of steely stratus clouds hung low in the autumn sky over the Missouri River and Omaha. A constant wind slowly pushed the continuous gray shelf east.

Gisele pulled her Accord up to the locked chain link gate at the back parking lot of The Ordinary. Her headlights illuminated lengths of yellow Caution tape fluttered in the breeze across the entrance.

Rich slept in the passenger seat. He'd been out since they went over the Mississippi River Bridge at Davenport.

"Richie?" She nudged his shoulder.

"Huh?" He woke with a start.

"We're here."

Rich wiped his eyes, blinked, stretched out his good arm and looked around. "Oh...okay, yeah."

"You have the remote opener?" Gisele asked.

Rich looked at her and laughed. "We're a pair."

Gisele's swollen right eye had turned from red to a purplish blue. She sported a world class shiner. A thick white bandage that went from the temple to the bridge of her nose was taped under her black eye. The changing fall weather coaxed her into wearing a heather zip sweatshirt over a black top with cream colored jeans.

"Speak for yourself." She brushed back her mid-length honey blonde hair from her high forehead.

"I don't have the remote. I'll go around to the front." Rich, his left arm in a sling, struggled out the passenger door. He walked stiffly down 16th street. A plywood board had been nailed over the window Nicky shot out. The bent nails showed it to be a hasty job. Turning the corner to Vinton Street Rich saw more yellow caution tape stretched across the front of The Ordinary. He fished for his keys with his free hand. Ducking under the crossed plastic tape, Rich crunched through broken glass strewn about the entrance. He unlocked the door and pushed it open.

Quiet and as cold as a tomb, Rich stepped into the dark insides of The Ordinary. It startled him. Most of the shot up tables and chairs, as well as the firework debris and brass casings scattered all over the floor, had not been cleaned up. The bar room smelled of stale beer, burn and something sour like turned milk. He looked behind the bar. The bodies were gone. He barked his shin on a table leg sticking out from a busted table as he picked his way through the blackness. A crazy mark with bullet holes stained the wall in the corner where Lavender had been. He felt along the top of the bar to the kitchen and back entrance. He pressed the open button on a wall mounted remote. He slid back the iron bar and unlocked the door, stepping out.

Gisele eased her Accord slowly into the lot, parking next to Rich's black F-150.

"Doesn't look so bad," Gisele said, climbing out. "You made it sound like all the windows and walls were blown to smithereens."

"You haven't seen the inside." Rich pressed the button, closing the chain link gate.

"You have to remember...I've never been here before." Gisele opened the trunk and took out her bag.

Rich pulled the back door closed behind him.

"Here's that satchel from the Mercury," Gisele said putting it on the gravel. "Am I glad I grabbed it when I did. The Feds were at my door wanting that car a couple of minutes after I got back from the emergency room."

"I'm glad you did too."

"I put your gun and phones in the satchel." Gisele picked up her bag. "Where do I go?"

"Upstairs." Rich picked up the black satchel with his right hand. "I'll get my rifle later." He slammed the trunk. "Did you say phones?" He wearily started up the iron stairs to the second floor.

Gisele followed, hand on the rusted rail. "Yeah. There were two phones on the front seat of the old car. I just threw them in the satchel."

Rich tore away the yellow tape from the door and sorted through his keys.

"Is this okay?" Gisele came up behind him.

He slipped the key in the lock and turned the doorknob. "Hell yeah, it's ours."

The door opened to a dim room with crooked shafts of streetlight from the windows falling on the floor and opposite wall. Rich stepped in. The quiet affected him. He missed hearing Roommate's greeting bark.

"Looks like The Cabinet of Dr. Caligari." Gisele peered over Rich's shoulder.

"It does not," he said, flipping on the kitchen light. He put the satchel on the stainless steel counter.

Gisele set her bag down and followed Rich through the apartment. The door jamb had bullet holes and long wood splinters sticking out. The living room was still a mess with the table overturned, chair and papers and laptop scattered about the floor. Rich picked up the lamp and turned it on. Light fell on a large oval brownish stain on the wood floor. The thick spot had cracks from drying out. In the center of the oval a hole rimmed in rough white wood went through the floor.

"Is that where?" Gisele pointed.

"It is," Rich pulled up from his gut with some difficulty. He stood staring down for a long while. Then, inhaling, turned away. He went over to the couch fully expecting to see Roommate laying there as if sleeping. "Wonder where Jorge put Roomy?"

"Did you tell him to take care of it?"

"I told him to put Roommate in a box. I would take care of him when I got back."

"This is a nice flat, Richie." Gisele started doing what women do, straightening things men had left in disarray. At a leisurely amble she went around and pulled blinds up and curtains across, righting the table, chair and putting the laptop and other papers on the top.

Nesting, Rich thought. He checked himself. Nesting sounded sarcastic. Gisele's presence gave him so much relief.

She straightened the picture of the two of them in Lahaina. "Oh, you have this picture. I thought we lost it. This's my favorite. Where's the bedroom?"

Rich retreated from his thoughts and motioned her toward the door, leading. The room looked okay when Rich turned the light on. Gisele brushed past him and sat bouncing on the bed.

"This is nice."

"Well, almost." Rich pointed to a line of bullet holes that went from the footboard of the bed to the wall. He looked up and saw matching holes in the ceiling. Speaking low he said: "Must've been when Yuri shot up the ceiling."

"We can patch those tomorrow. I like this room. It's really masculine." She fell back on the bed then jumped with a scream. "Something's in the bed."

Rich turned back the white comforter and there were four spent bullets on the sheet. He laughed and picked up the rounds. "No worry about bed bugs, Gis...just bed bullets."

"Are you going to be all right with me here?"

Rich turned and held her shoulder in his good hand. "Every night we were apart I dreamed of you here with me. The answer is yes. I want to know if you are going to be okay here after all that happened?"

"I can deal with anything now that we're together." They kissed. "But, where's the bathroom, I really need to go."

Rich pointed and off Gisele scrambled. He went back into the living room and heard Gisele talking from the bathroom.

"This bathroom looks like an Italian barbershop."

He opened the refrigerator and saw a large cardboard boot box and knew right away what it contained. Carefully he pulled the box out and put it on the counter. Stepping back, he looked at it.

"Can you turn the heat on? It's really chilly in here," Hugging herself, Gisele came up behind him. "Is that?"

"Yes." Rich lifted the lid. Inside a foggy wet plastic bag lay Roommate curled up as he had left him. Rich's lower lip and chin tensed.

"Oh honey, I'm sorry."

Rich closed the lid and put Roommate back in the refrigerator. "I'll deal with it tomorrow."

Gisele put her arm around him, kissing his neck.

Rich checked the laptop in the pantry. With a touch on the on/off button the screen came up showing all four surveillance cameras. He keyed in the archives and clicked back. Nicky's Mercury slid up 16th Street, stopping. They let someone out. Rich recognized Dedmon. He jogged across the street, disappearing from one screen. The Mercury turned left onto Vinton Street and drove out of the screen. Dedmon appeared at the back gate of The Ordinary. He tried to open the chain link gate. Nicky's Mercury made a U-turn on another screen and parked out front. Dedmon, unable to get in, walked to the front. He joined up with Nicky, Irina and Yuri getting out of the car.

In the living room he sorted through the piles on the table and found a thumb drive.

"What's that?" Gisele asked at the pantry door.

"The surveillance cameras picked up Nicky arriving at The Ordinary. I need to save it."

"Why?"

"In case the grand jury gets funky." He slipped the thumb drive in the USB port and copied, then pasted the archives to the drive. "Did you want to see the bar downstairs?"

"Tomorrow. Let's get something to eat and call it a day."

"Good idea. You want to go out?" Rich picked up the black satchel. "Wow, this thing is heavier than I thought. Did you look in it?"

"No, I just put your stuff in there. I saw the money, but didn't count it or anything."

Rich shook the satchel. "Sounds like there's change in the bottom." He lifted it onto the counter. "Let me put this drive away and I'll go down and see what Jorge has in the refrigerator. What're you hungry for?"

"Anything...well, no Mexican tonight, okay?"

Rich went into the living room and opened the gun safe. He put the thumb drive into the fat manila envelope with his notes. "Well, he probably has hamburger. Good for you?" He closed the heavy door, spinning the combination.

"That sounds great."

"There's wine in the 'fridge." Rich crossed to the dumb waiter in the pantry.

"I'll close my eyes," she said.

The light burned bright and white when Rich snapped it on in the kitchen. Glasses and plates, with half eaten sandwiches, were piled in the stainless steel sink. A box of taco shells lay open next to a cutting board with dried out diced tomatoes, wilted chopped lettuce, onions, cheese and avocado gone brown. Two bowls, with shredded chicken and ground beef were set before the microwave. These were Lt. Lavender's tacos. Rich opened the refrigerator. He tucked under his sling a bag of hamburger patties, condiments and buns.

"I got burger stuff," he called, climbing out the dumb waiter.

"I'll cook," Gisele took the patties and condiments from under Rich's sling. "I poured you a glass of wine."

Rich sat on a stool while Gisele turned to the stove. "Frying pan?"

"Under." Rich took a long drink of wine. He sighed, setting the glass down. "So you didn't look into the satchel?"

"Nope." She put two patties in the frying pan.

He unzipped the satchel and pulled out his Glock and shoulder holster. He put them to the side and peered in. "Honey, that's Nicky's phone. I forgot I had it. Boy, I bet some people would want to get their hands on that."

"Maybe you should give it to them?"

"I think I'll keep it for now. I can use it in my research and...if I need a bargaining chip." Rich pressed the power button. In a few seconds the screen came on. He scrolled through the contacts on Nicky's phone. "Wow. This could have the whole Bratva organization in Canada and the United States." The prompts were in Russian. He tried to find the picture Nicky took of him.

"Are the Russians going to come after you for that?"

"They won't know I have it." He put Nicky's phone next to the Glock.

"What about the FBI?" Gisele flipped the sizzling burgers.

"They probably don't know about it either." Rich took another drink of wine, staring at the phone. "They might figure it out then ask me if I have his phone."

Gisele pushed a plate in front of Rich and another for herself across from him. She refilled her glass of wine and sat. "I'm so hungry." She took a greedy bite.

"Thanks. Want to see what else is in Nicky's bag?"

"Mmmm," Gisele slid off her stool. "Let me get a pad." She went to the living room and came back with a pad and pen.

Between bites Rich took out rubber band bound bundles of old bills. He put out four piles for each currency: American, Canadian, Mexican and Russian rubles. Soon the pile of US currency grew twice as high as other nationalities.

"I think we have mostly greenbacks." Rich wiped his hands on a towel. "They don't feel clean." He took a packet. They were $20 bills. He fanned the bills. "There are 50 per pack, a $1000 each." The white backed Canadian currency was mostly $50s. The bundles were 25 bills per—about $2500 Canadian. Mexican pesos were in 100s. Rich counted a 100. That made 10,000 in pesos. As Rich got to the bottom of the satchel they could hear coins jingling.

"What's he got, honey, quarters?"

"For the car wash or laundromat, maybe?"

"Funny boy," Gisele dusted her fingers off and moved the pad closer. "What'd we got?"

Rich counted the stacks of US currency. "We have 26 packets of dollars."

"That's $26,000." Gisele made a note.

"And 16 Canadian."

Gisele gulped. "That's $100,000."

"It's Canadian, so probably about $75,000 American." Rich ate his last bite of hamburger. He almost giggled. "A million in pesos."

"Wow...what's that worth?"

"Dollar twenty, I think."

"Ha ha."

"I don't know the exchange rate, but I would guess at least 30 cents per peso. We're talking maybe $300,000." Rich picked up a packet of rubles. "Then these things. I have no idea what they're worth. Probably not much, what with all the international sanctions on the Russian economy."

"About a million dollars," Gisele gave Rich a wide-eyed, open mouth look.

"Yeah, but only the US dollars we can use."

"What do you mean?"

"Unloading the foreign bills would draw a lot of attention. Banks report that. The Treasury Department might come calling on the quick."

"What about the coins? They shouldn't be a problem."

Rich pulled the satchel closer, looking in. "Whoa."

"Whoa?" Gisele's face screwed up. "What's in there?"

Rich pulled one out. "It's gold. Not a US coin. Ever seen one of these, Gis?"

Gisele gasped. "It's a Krugerrand."

"What's that?"

"South African." She turned it over in her fingers, marveling. It gleamed in the light. "I have a client that puts most of his profit in gold. He buys Krugerrands. These are worth about $1200 each."

"There's hundreds of'em." Rich ran his fingers over the pile of coins at the bottom of the satchel.

"Let's go back to Lahaina."

Rich said nothing for a moment, staring into the satchel. "There's more stuff here."

"More money?"

"No." Rich threw some clothing to the floor and set out three rolled plastic baggies.

"Burn those clothes. What's in those bags?"

"This one's rocks." He held the bag up to the light. "This one is probably meth. And here's some weed."

"Keep the weed."

"Honey, we don't have time for that silly stuff." Rich unzipped a pocket in the satchel. "Holy crap, Gisele. He's got Russian, Canadian and Mexican passports. And this..." Rich opened a small 3 by 5 notebook. "...is like an address book." The black leather bound notebook, split at the spine, showed exposed cardboard at the corners. Rich thumbed through the brown-edged pages. Written in a small tight hand and mostly in Cyrillic, there were entries in English. He found Decker's name, address, a number and dollar sign. The book had contacts and clients for the whole of the sex operation run by Bratva in the Midwest.

"I would bet the insurance won't pay for all the damage. I'm okay with using the money for all the damage he did, but.... Are you listening to me?"

"Huh? Oh, yeah, I know. We can't keep some of this stuff. Let me think a second." Rich poured the last of the wine into his glass. Gisele got up, taking the plates and putting them in the sink. "I think I know what he was doing. Nicky planned on killing me. If he'd got away then he probably was heading south to lay low in Mexico. After a while he could come back through Canada. But here's what we're going to do."

Gisele fished out a cigarette from her purse. The lighter snapped a small blue flame. She blew a cloud of grey smoke toward the ceiling, then turned, folding her arms and leaning against the sink. Her narrow blondish brown brows knit together as she glared at the multi-colored stacks of foreign and American currency. Her good eye had a dark look and her face squeezed up as if disgusted. "Where'd this money come from?"

"It's not the church's take on weekly bingo."

"It's dirty. I don't want it."

"We'll keep the dollars. We can pay for repairs and bank them without drawing any attention. We'll take half the Canadian money and all the Krugerrands. We can put the Krugerrands in a safety deposit box." Rich drank. "The pesos, rubles and passports we're going to put back in the satchel and hand it over to the FBI."

"What about the drugs?"

"We could throw those in the satchel also."

"Aren't they going to wonder how we got the satchel?"

"Yeah. But we can tell them Nicky left it in the Mercury. We found it later."

"Don't you think they had crime scene people going over the car?"

"I do." Rich pinched his lower lip. "If Yuri or that young girl knew Nicky had a bag of money they'd tell the FBI. They'll know we took the money. But I don't think they'll care."

"What about that address book?"

"I'm keeping it." Rich put the small black book on Nicky's mobile phone.

"For your book?" She stared at him.

He smiled tightly in reply. "You know me too well."

"You piss off those people again and they'll send someone serious, not another nutball Russian hillbilly. I don't want to argue. I'm beat, babe," Gisele said. "Let's wrap it up and go snuggle in bed."

"You go. I'll put this stuff away and catch up to you."

With the dawn, Rich woke. Gisele lay curled next to him. Carefully, he slipped from under the bed clothes and quietly took his jeans, shirt and shoes from the chair. He dressed in the living room and went to the kitchen. Taking the cardboard box with Roommate from the refrigerator, he tucked the box under his sling and opened the back door.

If Rich had turned around he would've seen Gisele, who woke when he got out of bed, standing just back from the bedroom door, watching him.

The early morning air was crisp and cold. His breath came in steamy white gasps as he stepped down the iron stairs. A train whistle blew in the distance. Rich took a shovel from the tools under the stairs. Gisele's shadow showed at the back door. She was wrapped in the white comforter.

He took his arm out of the sling and dug into the hard cold dirt behind the dumpster with an anger that nearly bent the blade of the shovel. Once he penetrated the frozen surface he threw shovelful after shovelful into a pile. Though dressed in a t-shirt and jeans Rich still worked up a sweat digging the hole deep. Though his arm hurt, he dug. Putting the shovel aside Rich went down to his knees, placing the cardboard box into the bottom of the hole. With Gisele peering down, Rich bowed his head, silent for a long moment. The California Zephyr gave a short and long blast that faded to the east. Then he stood and quickly filled the hole with dirt. He wiped his eyes with his hands, replaced the shovel and started up the stairs.

Trying not to wake Gisele, Rich slipped off his shoes, pulled his shirt over his head and dropped his jeans. Glad he hadn't roused her and favoring his bad arm, he quietly as possible settled back into bed. She slept with her head on her arm. A strand of wavy honey blonde hair lay across the white bandage on her face. Rich sighed and closed his eyes. Had he opened his eyes he would've caught Gisele staring at him, a tear falling from her eye.

After breakfast Rich and Gisele went down to the bar room to start the cleanup. Gisele was appalled by the carnage of the bar room. "Oh my God, Rich—it looks like a bomb went off in here."

"Careful," Rich cautioned. "There's still a lot of glass and debris on the floor."

A plywood board covered the window. Bullet holes and gaping shotgun blasts were evident all over the walls and ceilings. The bar looked like it had been chewed and spit out by sharks. It stunk of smoke and blood. Rich got an acrid taste in the back of his mouth. In the far corner, stains marked the spot where Lavender sat. The big screen TV had a crooked line of holes from the lower corner to the top. Shredded fabric showed the paper cones inside shot out speakers. Pieces of tables and chairs were strewn about. Gisele stood dumbfounded. Rich went to the basement, returning with two full sized garbage cans and shovels.

"Here put these on." Rich handed Gisele a pair of leather work gloves. "Watch where you step."

"Where do we start?"

"You can start shoveling the glass and trash while I take the wrecked furniture out to the back."

"Okay."

Within a couple of hours they had cleared out the bar room and were starting on behind the bar.

Someone knocked on the door.

"Don't they know we're closed," Gisele said.

"I'll tell'em." Rich went to the door, unlocking and opening it.

On the sidewalk out front and dressed as if returning from mass at St. Bridget's stood Jorge, his wife Carmelita with their three daughters.

"*Senor Jefe*, you are back."

"Yes, Jorge." Rich pushed aside glass and a single bloody shoe from the entrance. "Come in. Come in."

Jorge wore pressed black jeans and a white western style snap button shirt embroidered with red roses. His long black hair was tied back. He ducked under the yellow caution tape and stepped in. Behind him entered Carmelita, shorter and wider than her husband. She wore a white dress and dark shawl. Her lush black hair framed her long distinguished face. The three girls also wore white dresses, with their hair done up as well. Isabel, the oldest, appeared as if put out by it all. She busied herself with her phone. Frida had wide eyes coming in and looking around. She seemed shaken. Little Jorgelina happily hopped in, all smiles.

Behind Jorge's family Rosella, Carmelita's sister, came in with a young man hanging off her shoulders.

"*Jefe*," Jorge began, taking Rich's hand. "*Mucho* sorry about *Senor* Tom and Roommate."

"Thank you, Jorge, Carmelita." Rich gave him a soul shake, then motioned over to Gisele. "I'd like to introduce Gisele."

"*La Jefa?*" He straightened to attention. "*Senora* Esslin is honor to meet you."

"*Mucho gusto*, Jorge...*Senora* Carmelita."

"Jorge, Gisele's my wife."

"You marry *La Jefa?*" Jorge drew back in surprise. "*Senora* Keeper?"

"No," Rich chuckled. "Gisele has been my wife all along."

Carmelita slapped her husband's arm. "I tole you. Dint I tole you?" She smiled sweetly up to Gisele.

"*Si.*" Jorge nodded, raising his eyes, silently entreating heaven for strength. He ushered the girls forward. "*Mi tres angels*—Isabel, Frida, little Jorgelina."

Each girl came forward with a courtesy. "Pleased to meet you *Senora*," they said.

Gisele smiled to Isabel and touched Jorgelina's cheek. Her small face beamed. Frida lifted her head. Her eyes were red from crying. "I, I really miss Roomy."

"Oh, I do too, sweetheart." Gisele stroked her black hair.

"Will we be open soon, *Jefe*?"

"Probably a week or two." Rich assured him. "In fact, I would like you to come this weekend and check the kitchen for any damage. You know, bullet holes in sink, pipes or appliances, like that."

"*Si si*, I do that."

"And Carmelita, once we open you and Rosella will go back on your usual cleaning schedule."

"*Gracias, Senora, Senor* Keeper." Carmelita clapped her hands and smiled.

"*Gracias*." Rosella echoed from behind.

"And you all are still on the payroll," Gisele added. Rich turned on her with a surprised expression. She continued, giving Rich a sideways look. "There will be no interruption with your paychecks."

"So wonderful, *gracias, gracias*."

Jorge lightly tapped his forehead and reached into his back pocket. "I forget almost, *Jefe*." He handed a business card to Rich. "Police, they give me this for you."

Rich held it up to the light. The card advertised a crime scene cleaning company. "Thanks, Jorge. I might just use this on some spots I don't want to touch."

"We go now. *Adios*. Is pleased to meet you *Senora*."

Rich saw Carmelita glance back. She loudly whispered: "*Senora* Keeper *es que bonita*."

Jorge and family went out the front door. Rosella followed and muttered "goodbye." Her boyfriend wagged his head and gave Rich a surly grin as he passed. Half a blurry number 13 tattoo showed above the collar of his shirt.

"You didn't have to keep them on the payroll," Rich said.

"It'll clean up some of that dirty money. I'd rather they put it to good use."

An hour later an Omaha Police patrol car parked out front. Two uniformed cops climbed out. They adjusted their caps and entered The Ordinary.

"Officers." Rich reached out his hand. "Thanks for stopping by." He shook the cop's beefy hand. "This is my wife, Gisele."

"M'am." The cop pinched the black visor of his cap.

The other cop squinted and moved his head to one side, admiring Gisele's black eye. "Wow. Lady, I have seen some shiners...but that is a humdinger."

"Thank you, I guess," Gisele replied.

"Bad guys do that to you?"

"Yes."

"How's Lt. Lavender?" Rich wanted to know.

"Have you seen him?"

"Not yet. We planned on going to Bergin Mercy Hospital later today."

"He's out of intensive care, but still critical."

"That's good news."

The cops nodded and walked around.

"Ow," a cop muttered. "I can still smell gun powder."

With his hand over his nose, the second cop added: "I know that other smell."

"This is like the inside of a brick of Swiss Cheese. It's a wonder anyone survived."

"Thank God the lieutenant did." Rich said.

"And you."

"I try not to think about that."

"We're going to have to get the lieutenant to tell us all about what happened."

"There's word the feds are going to put you up before a grand jury."

"Yeah, looks that way."

"I know the lieutenant would vouch for you. And I was here doing crowd control. I can tell'em it was like the Fourth of July in a phone booth."

"Thanks. I appreciate that."

"We got to get going. Glad you're getting back up and running."

"See you, officers. Thanks again for stopping in."

She stood in the entrance, a tall slender shadow. The cops excused themselves and went past. Rich knew right away.

"Honey." He touched Gisele's elbow.

She knew as well: "Daisy?"

"Yes."

Rich crossed the bar room to her and lead her in. She appeared disoriented and disheveled dressed all in black. In her hand she held a handkerchief, limp and wet from wiping her eyes. "You okay?" Rich asked with his arm around her shoulders.

"Huh?" She raised her head, unable to focus her eyes.

"Daisy, I'm Gisele." Moving from Rich's side, Gisele put her arm around Daisy's shoulders.

"Gisele? Tom talked about you a lot." Mentioning Tom brought forth a gush of tears. Gisele gave Rich the eye and walked Daisy to an undamaged table and chairs.

"I'll make some coffee," Rich said, going into the kitchen.

When he returned Daisy had her head down, the handkerchief over her eyes. Her shoulders shook. Gisele gently rubbed the young woman's shoulders. Rich put two cups of coffee on the table and went over to the bar.

Rich took out the card for the crime scene cleaning company. He called. A cheerful woman took down the information and scheduled a cleaning crew for the following day. Then Rich dialed the FBI office.

"FBI Omaha," a youngish sounding woman answered.

"Agent Paul Bertoloni, please."

"Who's calling?"

"Richard Rice."

"Please hold." Some sort of electronic mashup of bad music crackled over the connection. The girl came back on the line almost immediately. "I'm sorry, Agent Bertoloni is no longer at this office."

"What? What happened?"

"I have a note from Agent Bertoloni that if you called to refer you to the FBI's Chicago office."

"I'll be damned."

"Excuse me?"

"Oh nothing," Rich exhaled through his nose. "Did he leave a number to contact him?"

"I can transfer you to the Chicago office."

"Please do. Thanks."

The bad electronic music started up again.

"FBI Chi-caw-ga." An older woman with a pronounced New York accent answered.

"Agent Paul Bertoloni please."

"Who's caw-ling?"

"Richard Rice."

"Ho pleez." On an endless loop, the same electronic track started. "I'em sorry. I don't have an agent Ber-taw-loney."

"He just got transferred from Omaha."

"Ho pleez."

Rich watched Gisele comforting an almost inconsolable Daisy.

"Using your real name?" Bertoloni came on the line.

"Yeah. What'd you get promoted?"

"In a manner of speaking...yes."

"Not sure if I should congratulate you."

"I'll take that for a slap on the back. How's the wing?"

"It's all right. More of a nuisance than an injury. Ever try and perform your husbandly duties with your arm in a sling?"

"I'm not married."

"Tough luck for you." Rich shifted his tone. "Hey, listen, we found a black satchel in Nicky's Mercury."

"Oh really? What was in it?"

"You'll be interested. There are three passports, bags of dope and a pile of foreign money."

"What kinds?"

"Some weed, crack..."

"No...I meant the money."

Rich silently chuckled. "About a hundred thousand dollars Canadian. Maybe half that in Mexican pesos. And a slew of Russian rubles."

"No greenbacks?"

"Maybe a couple hundred bucks."

"A couple hundred?"

"Yeah, about that."

A silence fell over the line.

Bertoloni audibly sighed. "All right...about a hundred dollars. Anything else?"

Rich realized he had to make a choice, the address book or Nicky's phone. He wasn't going to surrender the address book. "No." He baited the hook.

"No?" Bertoloni paused. "Didn't you have Nicky's phone?"

"Oh, I did. I took it with me to Glencoe. I thought I left it in the Mercury."

"We didn't find it." And he slowly, deliberately said: "You sure you don't have Nicky's phone?"

"Not on me." Rich played out his line, gently jiggling the sparkling lure. "You think there's information on Nicky's phone?"

"That's not what I mean."

"I don't know what you meant."

Neither spoke for a moment.

"I'll tell you what," Bertoloni started in a hard tone. "You look around. You take a real good look around again and see if maybe you can find Nicky's phone. I'll have an agent out there tomorrow for that bag. I hope Nicky's phone is in that bag."

Strike, Rich started to reel him in. "I'll have a look. I might find it."

"Son of a bitch, Rich, you can't fuck with us like this."

"You fucked with me and got yourself a big promotion." And he landed him.

Bertoloni had no response.

"Tell me. Did you catch Suka before she made it to Canada?"

"I can't comment on an ongoing investigation."

"Slick...ongoing means you didn't catch her."

"I can't comment." Bertoloni sounded smug.

"As long as she's out there I'm not safe, nor is Gisele."

"I can't comment."

"And as long as Suka's out there you got a cushy job and can move up the pay grades."

"I can't comment." Bertoloni's voice verged on exasperation.

"Send your agent out. If I find Nicky's goddamn phone you can shove it up your ass."

"Pleasure as always, Rich."

"It never ends, does it, Bertoloni?"

Rich clicked off. He took a deep breath. Gisele looked up from talking to Daisy.

"What's up?" She walked over.

"Nothing..."

"Is it okay if Daisy stays with us tonight? She can sleep on the couch." Gisele glanced back at the crestfallen girl. "I don't think she should be alone."

"Fine. Listen, I have to do something."

"Okay. Do what you need to do."

Rich went upstairs and took Nicky's phone. With the butt of his Glock he shattered the face of the phone. He dropped it in the black satchel. He fanned through the address book. No telling how useful the names, addresses would be. Rich bagged up the dollars and Krugerrands and put them in the gun safe. Gisele came in with Daisy and led her into the living room. Rich put the address book on the counter and set the Glock on it. Gisele spread a comforter over Daisy as she lay on the couch.

"That poor girl hasn't slept in days." She said coming into the kitchen. "I heard parts of your conversation with the FBI guy. The bullshit's not over, is it?" Gisele crossed her arms and stared at Rich a long time.

Rich couldn't look at her. He had no reply.

ABOUT THE AUTHOR

Cort Fernald is a professional writer with newspaper and magazine publishing credits spanning more than 30 years. Cort has written news, features and editorials for a variety of publications.

In 2013 Cort published his first novel *Algonquin*. *Algonquin* is available through retail outlets and other retailers. *Sisters' Secret,* his second novel, was published in 2014. *Keeper of an Ordinary* is his third novel.

Cort holds a degree in English from Southern Oregon University, and did graduate work in journalism at the University of Oregon. A member of the Nebraska Writers Guild and Nebraska Writers Workshop, Cort currently resides in Omaha, Nebraska.

ALGONQUIN by Cort Fernald

When Royce Partridge learns his boyhood pal Toby Bergman is dying of cancer he returns to the small town of Algonquin, Illinois on the Fox River where they grew up. Royce left Algonquin 40 years ago. Progress in the form of strip malls, subdivisions and congested traffic, has changed the once bucolic river town. Royce surprises Toby in the hospital and slipping fast. Royce stays in Algonquin at a quaint Victorian bed & breakfast.

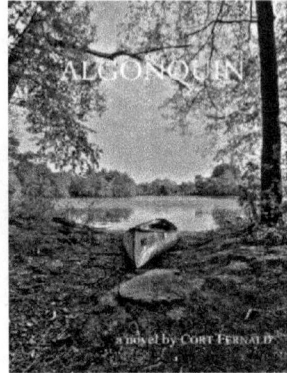

Despite of the heavy hand of progress Royce can see the small town he and Toby raced mopeds around as teenagers. But it is down on the banks of the Fox River that Royce relives the wild adventure he, Toby and two other friends had the summer of 1964 before they started high school.

Available from retail and internet retailers, as well as www.cortbooks.com

SISTERS' SECRET by Cort Fernald

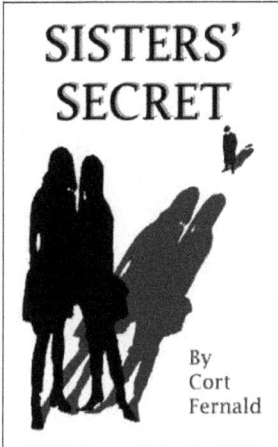

Sisters' Secret is a novel of grief and obsession. Mike Smith's beloved wife, Rebecca, is raped and murdered by unknown assailants. The police haven't a clue. Mike tries to lose himself in his work. He tries to get on with his life. Months later, he attends his high school reunion. There he learns his high school girlfriend and her younger sister were abducted and gang raped. The crime was never reported.

Mike is horrified, but moreover, he believes he knows who among his classmates committed this crime.

Mike sets out to expose the criminals. But in so doing, he puts his life at risk

Available from retail and internet retailers, as well as www.cortbooks.com